LEADERSHIP
FOR
WOMEN
IN·THE
CHURCH

Foreword by
Dr. D. James Kennedy

LEADERSHIP
FOR
WOMEN
IN·THE
CHURCH

SUSAN HUNT &
PEGGY HUTCHESON

ZONDERVAN™

GRAND RAPIDS, MICHIGAN 49530 USA

ZONDERVAN™

Leadership for Women in the Church
Copyright © 1991 by Susan Hunt and Peggy Hutcheson

Requests for information should be addressed to:

Zondervan, *Grand Rapids, Michigan 49530*

Library of Congress Cataloging-in-Publication Data

Hunt, Susan M., 1940-
    Leadership for women in the church / Susan M. Hunt and
Peggy G. Hutcheson.
      p. cm.
    ISBN 0-310-54021-6
    1. Christian leadership.   2. Women in church work.   I. Hutcheson,
Peggy G.   II. Title.
BV652.H77 1991
253'.082—dc20   91-21390
                                                  CIP

Cover design by Gary Gnidovic

Printed in the United States of America

---

10 11 12 /DC/ **19**

To our husbands
Gene Hunt
and
Ware Hutcheson
We thank God for designing us to be your helpers...
We thank you for making that such a fulfilling life adventure!

A Leader's Guide is available from the Presbyterian Church in America bookstore: 1-800-283-1357

Contents

Foreword   9

Introduction   10

Acknowledgments   13

PART ONE
THE CHALLENGES OF LEADERSHIP

CHAPTER ONE
The Issues   17

CHAPTER TWO
The Biblical Ideal   25

CHAPTER THREE
The Qualities   35

CHAPTER FOUR
The Arena   43

PART TWO
THE ELEMENTS OF LEADERSHIP

CHAPTER FIVE
Focus   57

CHAPTER SIX
Wisdom   73

CHAPTER SEVEN
Confidence   97

CHAPTER EIGHT
Unity   117

Conclusion   136

Foreword

Since the formation of the Presbyterian Church in America in 1973, an impressive flow of significant literature has emanated from its ranks in a steadily increasing volume. *Leadership for Women in the Church* is an outstanding example of the high quality of such bibliographical output.

Susan Hunt and Peggy Hutcheson provide a valuable combination of practical church experience and professional credentials. Together, they achieve that goal of handling a serious treatise in a manner that reflects deep and dedicated scholarship, yet almost entertaining the reader with the sprightly style of expression apparent from the opening chapter and throughout the book.

By outlining a clear goal under each chapter title, and following that up with a life example and a fascinating illustration of the specific contribution to spiritual understanding made by selected women of the Bible, the authors are able to explain with great clarity the ways in which women bring to church fellowship and ministry a vitality and a completeness that are indispensable in the body of Christ.

I believe that this work will prove to be of special value when used as a text. It brings into marvelous focus the scriptural concept of the vital role of women in the church, and because of its frank and comprehensive approach to its subject, the book will appeal to both men and women seeking to understand one of the most important aspects of healthy church life.

I find this volume delightful. It is my conviction that many readers of *Leadership for Women in the Church* will share my view.

D. James Kennedy
Coral Ridge Presbyterian Church
Fort Lauderdale, Florida

Introduction

This book is about how Christian women can identify and focus their leadership skills on tasks that need to be undertaken in the church. It is about how Christian men can recognize and use the leadership talents of the women in the church. Finally, it is about how local churches, those with denominational affiliation and those without, can integrate the full range of women's abilities with the tremendous needs in the kingdom of God.

This book is not about justifying the position of male headship or about the issue of ordination of women to offices of authority within the church. We (Peggy and Susan) accept the teaching of our church in these matters. (You may want to review *Man and Woman in Biblical Perspective* by James Hurley for an exposition of this position.) Rather, we are attempting to address creatively the issue of how women function within a church where male headship is the accepted position.

We write out of the realization that our personal pilgrimages for the last fifteen years have solidified our adherence to the position of male headship in the church. We are increasingly convinced of the theological rightness of this position. But the more urgent motivation is to help Christians move beyond confusion and debate over our roles toward active concern about the needs around us. We are convinced that the church provides that most appropriate context for Christian women to serve the Savior. We further contend that rather than being *restrained by* our exclusion from ordination, women are actually *freed from the restraints* of positions of authority to be exquisite expressions of the biblical meaning of a helper-leader. When women insist on role interchangeability within the church, everyone loses. But when women are creatively giving spiritual, emotional, and practical help, they add a unique and vibrant dimension that permeates an entire church fellowship and brings completeness to its ministry.

That's what the book is about, but the why lies in a passion we share. We are two women with many "parts" to our lives. We are wives, mothers, and daughters. One of us (Susan) is a grandmother. One of us (Peggy) is president of the board of a chamber music group. We are active members of our respective churches, and we both have careers. We are both, along with our husbands, avid football fans. We enjoy full lives. So why take on another project? Because this shared passion is an intense desire to see Christian women recognize and develop their potential in Christ, and to see the church unleash this "feminine power" for kingdom service. Throughout history women have been the molders of culture. This is reflected in the statement, "The hand that rocks the cradle is the hand that rules the world,"* but is more powerfully stated in Scripture, "The wise woman builds her house, but with her own hands the foolish one tears hers down" (Prov. 14:1). Obviously this verse is not talking about the physical structure of a house but about the character of the people in that house. Our culture is in danger. We felt propelled to write this book because we believe that women can make a difference.

In today's world it is more and more evident that things are done well where there is good leadership. It is also evident that the kind of leadership most called for today is not leadership in the traditional sense of "management." Whether in business,

---

*William Ross Wallace (1819–1881), *The Hand That Rules the World.* Stanza 1.

nonprofit service organizations, or religious organizations, leadership calls for people to use their gifts to the fullest, developing their interpersonal skills and influence skills, so that they can get things done even when they have no formal authority. Effective leaders are able to formulate clear visions of what needs to be accomplished, organize others to believe in and support those visions, mobilize resources to action, and build relationships for continued progress. Leaders do not necessarily function from a base of formal authority or a position of power. Their effectiveness comes from their abilities to develop followers—contributors to the shared goals of the group. This means that leaders are helpers, too, finding ways to support others as everyone works together toward goals that are far too big to be undertaken by one or even a few.

This book is intended to present information about leadership and about the issues that women face today in ways that free women to contribute more of their talents to their local churches. We believe this freedom comes when we stop equating leadership with positional power or authority. This book is for women, but it is also for men. It is for everyone who is willing to accept the challenge to think about women's roles and contributions in churches today.

Throughout this book, we will be speaking directly to you, our readers. We believe that the content of the book is a personal message, and we want to talk directly to you. In a few cases, there are personal examples or expressions that truly do belong to just one of us. In these cases, we will indicate which of us is speaking.

Finally, keep in mind that God's glory is the theme of this book. Psalm 34:3 is our theme text: "Glorify the Lord with me; let us exalt his name together." We believe that there are ideas within these pages that can free Christian women and Christian men to more fully glorify him. We pray that, as you read each chapter, you will seek and find a creative stimulus, rather than points of dissension.

Acknowledgments

Writing this book has been a joint venture of those people who make up the "support system" that we value and appreciate. We want to acknowledge all of you, however, we cannot mention everyone who has contributed. Some of you will find your names mentioned here. We hope that others of you will mentally add your names because we do appreciate your support and guidance.

FROM SUSAN

In addition to Gene, my greatest supporters are our children: Kathryn and Dean Barriault, Richie and Shannon Hunt, and Laurin Hunt. They have prayed, and they have been patiently flexible! My mother, Mary Kathryn McLaurin, as always, has been a true helper. The women in my church, Midway Presbyterian, have been model encouragers. I am also grateful to the members of the Women In the Church Advisory Committee for the Presbyterian Church in America. These women have been my cheerleaders. The Christian Education staff of the Presbyterian Church in America, where I work, have been wonderful. I am especially grateful to Jane Brooks, my friend, co-laborer, and prayer partner. In addition to being coworkers in the field of Christian Education, Charles Dunahoo, Bob Edmiston, and Allen Curry have been faithful pastor-teachers as they have helped me shape a biblical approach to life. Their prodding has pushed me to examine everything in light of God's Word, and I am thankful for their leadership and support.

FROM PEGGY

I am grateful for all the women who have shown me such a variety of approaches to leadership. My mother, Martha Godwin, taught me how to lead from behind. My grandmother, Ruth Godwin, showed an ever-increasing dependence on God, not as a weakness, but as a strength. My colleagues in business have shown how Christian women can model their faith without sacrificing their effectiveness in the workplace. I am especially grateful to Susan McClure and Rebecca Padgett for this. The most important women who are currently in my life, my children Anne and Laura, model encouragement—even when my work makes things more difficult for them. I am grateful, too, for all the men and women whose teaching and guidance continue to contribute to my spiritual growth. What I have learned from Gene Hunt, Dale Welden, Richard Smith, Ross Cook, and others has guided and challenged me to align every aspect of life, not with the world's expectations, but with God's truths. Direct contributions to this book came from my coworkers at Atlanta Resource Associates: Sheila Thomas, Jack Watts, and Nancy Brigman. I am thankful both for what they have contributed and for the open, enthusiastic way they have offered their help.

PART ONE

THE CHALLENGES
OF LEADERSHIP

CHAPTER ONE

The Issues

1

Glorify the LORD with me: let us exalt his name together (Psalm 34:3).

GOAL: To present the complex questions about roles and the related issues facing women and men in evangelical churches.

"I have to admit that I leave meetings like this feeling frustrated and not really appreciated. I feel put down by a group of men who seem to be patting me on the head and saying, 'We'll take over now.'" Christy was cautiously revealing her annoyance, and I had to admit that I could understand her feelings. She had worked so long to raise the consciousness of members of her church to a particular need. At first, no one seemed to share her burden. Then the issue became a "hot item" and suddenly everyone was concerned. The male leadership of the church became involved and organized a meeting to decide how to meet the need. Christy was given a few minutes on the agenda, but the men were clearly the "movers and shakers."

If you asked Christy, she would tell you that she usually has no problems with the traditional biblical interpretation of male headship. But somehow, at times like this when the idea of headship is put into practice, traditional views of headship just do not "fit" for her. The elders of the church were the only ones in the position to make decisions; yet if you had added up their collective knowledge on this issue, it would not even have begun to approach Christy's expertise.

"This issue is a big one to me," Christy lamented, "My heart is in it, and I've been gathering information and working on it for more than a year! They asked me to give them some background on the issue. They also suggested that, since I was concerned about making sure things went smoothly for the meeting, I take charge of the nursery and fellowship time. Then what do they do? The meeting ended with three elders being appointed to do more study."

As we listen to Christy, some important questions come to mind. . .

- Can the traditional evangelical church offer women challenging, significant opportunities to serve?
- Is there a place in the local evangelical church for women who have gifts, training, and experience as executives, planners, implementers, etc.?
- If so, is it possible to maintain biblical male headship in the church and employ the nontraditional leadership abilities of women?
- Is the church an appropriate place for women to develop and exercise leadership skills?
- How does the church use the gifts of stay-at-home moms, empty nesters, and great-grandmothers and encourage these women to develop new skills?
- How can women in various seasons and circumstances of life experience oneness as they grow and serve Christ together in the church?
- What responsibility does the church have to deal creatively with these issues?

The Christian woman today is confronted with many perplexing issues. One of these is the question of her role in the church. Determining how she functions in her local church poses both problems and possibilities for the woman who believes that the Bible is the infallible, authoritative Word of God and who holds to the male-headship role in the church.

Too often because of confusion over the role of women in the local church, it is problems rather than possibilities that surface. Consequently, the female population remains an important untapped resource in most churches. Many evangelical leaders agree that one of the most important challenges the church faces in the 1990s is to recognize women's gifts and free the women to exercise them.

We would add that evangelical women face the challenge to speak boldly and clearly on the role of Christian women in the home and church. We hear that this is the decade of women, but we must not allow the world's voices to set the agenda for the church. We must unashamedly articulate and model the biblical position of male headship on this crucial issue. In order to seize this exciting opportunity, men and women must extend their theological *position* on the issue to the *practice* of that position. The position has been stated and restated! Now let's do some creative thinking about putting our beliefs into practice.

Men and women who have attached themselves to evangelical churches that do not ordain women to the position of pastor or elder seem to face a confusing dilemma. There is a tension for those who hold the position that the Bible teaches that women *are not to be ordained* to positions of authority, but who also hold that all believers are to discover and *exercise their gifts* for the good of the church. Can women obey both of these truths? If so, how do Christian women identify and focus their leadership abilities on tasks and opportunities within the church? How do Christian men in leadership positions recognize the gifts of women and integrate the full range of abilities that today's women have with the tremendous needs in the kingdom of God? We believe that this tension can be resolved and these questions answered without capitulating to those who insist that equal ministry opportunities for women demand ordination for women.

The issue is more complicated in today's evangelical

church because of the increasing variety of skills that women possess. Christian women whose gifts are being developed in the business world, who function as managers and professionals directing the activities of others in their work lives, wonder how they can achieve this same level of contribution in their church lives. In many churches, the only opportunities for women to be involved in ministry are in the domestic areas. It is not that these women are unwilling to keep the nursery and plan fellowship suppers, nor do they view these tasks as insignificant. However, because of lack of experience in these areas, they feel insecure and inadequate. They long for opportunities to serve in situations where they can utilize their abilities and experiences to make contributions within their congregations. Yet they do not know what is appropriate. They do not want to appear pushy so they do nothing—and that leads to a stifled, frustrated feeling.

Many women who excel in the domestic area also feel confused because frequently their contributions to their churches do not seem to be valued and appreciated. Women who are accomplishing great things in the roles they play in the women's groups in their churches wonder why their ideas seem to be less valuable than do men's in the overall functioning of the church. The women who lead the women's ministries, keep the nursery, and prepare the meals are seldom given the same recognition as the men who teach adult Bible classes or who serve as officers and pastors. Tasks traditionally delegated to women are too often taken for granted and not viewed as significant ministry. This, too, leaves women feeling stifled and frustrated.

The confusion is also intensified because women are usually not involved in the decision-making process in a church. In most evangelical churches, decisions are made by men ordained to offices of authority. Few churches have taken the time to creatively employ women as well as unordained men in the process of decision making.

For many women, this is not necessarily a raging frustration. They do what needs to be done. But there is an

22

undercurrent of discontent, a feeling of being unfulfilled within the church. Many find opportunities for significant ministry outside the church. Their energies, experiences, and leadership are lost to their local fellowships. There is nothing wrong with giving a portion of our time and abilities to outside-the-church work, yet God's people are commanded to use their spiritual gifts within the church "for the common good" (1 Cor. 12:7). Women who have a love for the church will not, and should not, be satisfied with pouring all their energies into outside ministry opportunities. This is where shared responsibility comes into play. Women are responsible for using their abilities for the good of their local churches. The churches are responsible for employing the gifts of all their members.

As theological debates about "women's issues" occur in denominations and Christian publications, the local church leadership is faced with the at-hand, practical matter of recognizing and releasing the gifts of women. We wonder whether all the confusion is simply a device of the enemy of the church to divert our attention away from the tremendous needs both within and outside the church. There are hurting people within the church, and there is a world outside the church that is falling apart. Because women are such relational creatures, with the God-given capacity to love and nurture hurting people, it should not surprise us that this is the segment of the Christian population that Satan seeks to immobilize through the tactic of confusion.

The theological questions and the frustrations of women are not to be taken lightly, but it is time for evangelical women to move beyond confusion to active concern. Confusion about our role in the church is a tactic Satan uses to keep us from involved concern regarding the needs around us. The leadership abilities of every member of the kingdom are urgently needed. There is too much kingdom work to be done.

How do women who want to serve through the ministry of their church move beyond confusion to active, involved concern? That's what this book is about. We will begin by developing the concept of women as helper-leaders. Then we

23

will translate this concept into practice through life situations. We believe this concept can form the basis of any women's ministry in any church, or the personal philosophy of any woman who is struggling with serving in a fulfilling, appropriate way within her church. Our starting point is the beginning—the creation of Eve.

CHAPTER TWO

The Biblical Ideal

2

Glorify the LORD with me: let us exalt his name together (Psalm 34:3).

> The LORD God said, "It is not good for the man to be alone. I will make a helper suitable for him" (Gen. 2:18).

GOAL: To show how the biblical role of helper is a positive, powerful role; and to help men and women go beyond narrow role definitions to focus on our ultimate purpose.

God created the woman to be a helper for the man. It is no mistake that God made Adam alone and incomplete. God made Adam incomplete because he intended to create a "completer." The presence and the ministry of a helper were necessary before God gave the pronouncement, "It is good." Is not the same true in the church? Surely the supportive ministry of women is as crucial to give completeness to the local church as was Eve's presence in the Garden. God made the pronouncement, "It is not good" regarding Adam's incompleteness. Is it stretching our imaginations too much to believe that he might also say, "It is not good" to a church that is not employing the gifts of women?

Before we develop the idea of women as helpers, we want to be sure you do not hear us saying something we are not saying. In no way do we mean to imply that the function of a helper is outside the realm of male responsibility. Mutual support and help among all believers is a basic scriptural principle. However, Genesis 2:18 does say that the woman was uniquely created as a helper for the man, and we believe that this has exciting implications for women as they function within the church.

If you are feeling uncomfortable with the role of being a completer or a helper, you are probably not alone. Is this relegating women to an inferior role? Before deciding, look at some other references in the Old Testament where "ezer," the Hebrew word for helper, is used.

> . . .My father's God was my helper; he saved me from the sword of Pharaoh. (Ex. 18:4)
>
> May he send you help from the sanctuary and grant you support from Zion! (Ps. 20:2)
>
> We wait in hope for the LORD; he is our help and our shield. (Ps. 33:20)
>
> Surely God is my help; the LORD is the one who sustains me (Ps. 54:4)
>
> Yet I am poor and needy; come quickly to me, O God. You are my help and my deliverer; O LORD, do not delay. (Ps. 70:5)
>
> Give me a sign of your goodness, that my enemies may see it and be put to shame, for you, O LORD, have helped me and comforted me. (Ps. 86:17).
>
> Blessed is he whose help is the God of Jacob, whose hope is in the LORD his God. . . . (Ps. 146:5)

These passages, like many others in the Old Testament, refer to God as our helper. They clearly show that the role of helper is not an inferior role. If we devalue the supportive ministry of help, we devalue the importance of God's ministry of help to us!

Men and women do have different roles in the family and in

28

the church. This does not mean superior-inferior roles. Our ministry opportunities should not be hindered because of this difference. In fact, ministry should be enhanced and made complete through our different roles. When we attach degrees of value to these roles, we set the stage for competition and discontent.

The Godhead gives us an example of difference in function but equality in existence. There are various roles within the Trinity. Yet we know that the Father, Son, and Holy Spirit are "the same in substance, equal in power and glory" (Westminster Shorter Catechism, Q. 6). Ontologically (relating to existence) there is equality in the Trinity, but economically (relating to function) there are different roles. If this is true in the Trinity, we certainly should be comfortable with different male and female roles within the church.

God clearly tells us that "There is neither. . .male nor female, for you are all one in Christ Jesus" (Gal. 3:28): Ontological equality.

God just as clearly tells us that ". . .the head of every man is Christ, and the head of the woman is man. . ." (1 Cor. 11:3): Economical difference.

If you have any lingering frustration with being created to be a helper, or if you still believe that being a helper limits the use of a woman's gifts or assigns to her a weaker role, look again at the Scripture references and consider *how* God himself is our helper.

God helps his people by protecting, supporting, shielding, sustaining, delivering, comforting, giving hope, and blessing. God's ministry of help is described in connection with action words indicating great strength. Being a helper is neither a lesser role nor a weaker role. Helping is certainly not a passive role.

Women have been created and equipped to be helpers—to lovingly protect, support, shield, sustain, deliver, comfort, give hope, and bless. To carry out this undergirding, supportive ministry, women need spiritual strength and security. They do not need confusion about their role. The first step out of

29

confusion into strength and security is an understanding of that most basic issue, our reason for being. God has spoken clearly on this issue: "Bring my sons from afar and my daughters from the ends of the earth—everyone who is called by my name, whom I created for my glory, whom I formed and made" (Isa. 43:6b–7).

The Christian's objective should be God's glory. David came to this conclusion and expressed it beautifully:

> I will extol the LORD at all times;
>   his praise will always be on my lips.
> My soul will boast in the LORD;
>   let the afflicted hear and rejoice.
> Glorify the LORD with me:
>   let us exalt his name together. (Ps. 34:3)

David was not trying to "find himself." He was beyond any confusion about his role or his identity. The theme of his life was God's glory. The Westminster Divines cut right to the bottom line when they say, "The chief end of man is to glorify God and to enjoy Him forever" (Westminster Shorter Catechism, Q. 1).

A bright, searching young woman once asked me, "Was it not egotistical of God to create us for his glory?" This was an honest, legitimate question of one seeking to understand the purpose of her existence. She listened intently as I explained that it was not God's ego that caused him to create us for his glory. God does not need us to glorify him in order to be glorified! God is glorious in and of himself—the very heavens shout forth his glory (Ps. 19:1). He created us to reflect his glory because of *our* need, not *his* need. There is no other purpose that would have given us significance. Being created to reflect the glory of the Creator elevates us to a position of potential power in a way that nothing else could do. This power can only be realized when we are resurrected from spiritual death by the grace of Jesus Christ.

When God's glory is our reason for being, we are freed from the entanglements of self-interest, self-promotion, and self-centeredness. We are freed from the domination of sin and liberated for our primary purpose. Freedom from the rule of sin releases the potential for which we were created—to reflect the glory of the Glorious One. Women reflect this glory by obeying the Master Designer's plan and offering all of their gifts to serve him.

Not until we have committed ourselves to the objective of God's glory and attached enormous value to that objective are we willing to be helpers; giving assistance and support to others. Unless our attention is riveted on God's glory, one of three things happens:

- We begin focusing on the person we are helping and eventually become discouraged with them;
- We begin looking at the difficulty of our situation and develop a sense of hopelessness;
- We begin focusing on ourselves and eventually self-interest creates a conflict.

We are only freed to serve as helpers when we can look beyond the limitations of those we are helping, the frustrations of our personal situations, and the selfish desires of our own hearts. Then we can focus on the real issue—God's glory. Unless our "chief end" is to glorify God, we quickly lose our capacity as well as our desire to be helpers and we disqualify ourselves from being leaders in God's church. A helper-leader must be focused on glorifying God.

Another obstacle in the way of our being absorbed with God's glory is that women often define their identities in terms of their roles, abilities, circumstances, or opportunities in life. The woman who succumbs to this is as unsteady and fragmented as her identity appears to be at any given moment. The result is tremendous confusion. When our reference point is the glory of God, and our ultimate definition of ourselves is as a child of the King, then our roles, abilities, circumstances, and opportunities no longer limit us. Rather, they become a means of fulfilling our purpose. What would be considered a limitation by the world actually becomes a platform for the believer—a platform to display the glory of God.

31

Glorifying God as a helper-leader is no easy task. We need great energy, humility, and wisdom to keep our attention fastened on God's glory. We must constantly choose to obey truth rather than listen to the lie of the enemy. This ongoing battle between God's glory and *my* ideas, *my* agenda, *my* interest is fierce spiritual warfare. It should be recognized as such.

It is difficult for anyone to deny self and give glory to another. This is just not natural. Glorifying God means ceasing to glorify self. Glorifying God is the essence of humility, and Jesus gave us the perfect pattern that we are commanded to follow.

> Your attitude should be the same as
> that of Christ Jesus:
>
>   Who, being in very nature God,
>   did not consider equality with
>   God something to be
>   grasped,
>   but made himself nothing,
>   taking the very nature of a
>   servant,
>   being made in human likeness.
>   And being found in appearance as a
>   man,
>   he humbled himself
>   and became obedient to death—
>   even death on a cross!
>   Therefore God exalted him to the
>   highest place
>   and gave him the name that is
>   above every name,
>   that at the name of Jesus every knee
>   should bow,
>   in heaven and on earth and under
>   the earth,
>   and every tongue confess that Jesus
>   Christ is Lord,
>   to the glory of God the Father. (Phil. 2:5–11)

He had to become empty to be exalted.

32

What delight the Father took in his Son! But God's love letter to us tells us that he also takes delight in and exalts his people. "For the LORD takes delight in his people; he crowns the humble with salvation. Let the saints rejoice in this honor and sing for joy on their beds" (Ps. 149:4–5).

It is the believer who has relinquished all claim to self who is crowned with salvation. It is the believer who rejoices in the honor of salvation—not the honor of position—who delights and glorifies the Father. And this believer is no longer confused. She is ready to focus her concerns on the needs around her.

When we come to the place of recognizing that the very purpose of our existence is to glorify God and we yield to his rule in our lives, then we enter the privileged calling of being a helper-leader. It is not easy. It is not natural. This discipline requires supernatural intervention. The Spirit-empowered life of obedience is nourished as we feed on God's Word. We must be women of the Word—women who *think* biblically so that we will *act* biblically, regardless of the pressures and voices of our culture.

Our Heavenly Father tells us that "The wise woman builds her house, but with her own hands the foolish one tears hers down" (Prov. 14:1). It is a woman of great wisdom who abandons herself to God's glory as the driving force of her life. This woman energetically and creatively lives out her reason for being. She has a powerful, positive influence—a "building" influence—on those around her. She glorifies God by protecting, supporting, shielding, sustaining, delivering, comforting, giving hope, and blessing those around her. Families, the church, and the world are in desperate need of these women. The Proverbs 31 composite of a noble, wise woman describes a helper-leader and then concludes that those affected by her ministry "arise and call her blessed."

Phoebe, a New Testament woman, must have been just such a helper-leader in her church, for the apostle Paul "arose and called her blessed" when he wrote to the church in Rome, "I commend to you our sister Phoebe, a servant of the church in Cenchrea. I ask you to receive her in the Lord in a way worthy of the saints and to give her any help she may need from you, for she has been a great help to many people, including me" (Rom. 16:1–2).

What a legacy for Christian women!

This leadership legacy may seem to be paradoxical. How can a helper be called a leader? And how can a leader be a helper?

34

CHAPTER THREE

The Qualities

3

*Glorify the LORD with me: let us exalt his name
together* (Psalm 34:3).

Those who are wise will shine like the brightness of the
heavens, and those who lead many to righteousness,
like the stars for ever and ever (Dan. 12:3).

GOAL: To show how leadership emerges from the qualities of
the leader, not from formal positions of authority.

These questions—how can a helper be called a leader?
And, how can a leader be a helper?—are much easier to answer
once we separate leadership from another term that is often
confused with it—management. In today's world it is more and
more evident that things get done when there is leadership. It is
also evident that the kind of leadership most called for is not
what is traditionally thought of as management.

Traditional management draws its power from the official
position of the manager. This position of power establishes the
manager as "the one who calls the shots." Managers plan,
organize, delegate, and control. Managers direct others. They do
this so that they accomplish the single function that manage-

ment is all about—motivating others to do the work. The workers under these managers are often referred to as subordinates. In traditional management, one person is clearly set apart as being more important than the others.

This traditional managerial approach is still alive in many organizations today. More and more, however, we are finding that the complexity of today's world, coupled with increased access to information, and the ready availability of talent, creates an environment in which other management styles are more effective.

What is taking the place of traditional management today? Traditional managers are being replaced by people who have a different approach to getting things done. Management is being replaced by leadership. Leaders are able to influence others even when they have no formal authority. Leaders are able to visualize clearly what needs to be accomplished. They are able to organize others to believe in and support this vision, mobilize the resources to get action, and build relationships for continued progress. Leaders work well in informal (unstructured), as well as formal (structured) organizations. They are a much-needed asset on committees. They may serve in elected or appointed positions. Wherever they are, leaders do not rely on a base of formal authority or a position of power. Their effectiveness comes from their abilities to develop followers—contributors to the shared goals of the group.

Management entails getting things done *through* others. Leadership is more aptly defined as getting this done *with* others. If, as many believe, leadership equals influence, all Christian women have the opportunity to influence others. In the roles of wives, mothers, daughters, and friends we influence through our words and our lives.

Leaders have at least four qualities that separate them from managers. These qualities can enable the Christian woman to influence those around her to follow the One she follows, and thus she will lead them to righteousness.

VISION: The first quality that leaders possess is vision. Leaders focus on possibilities. These possibilities (sometimes called goals or dreams) guide the decisions and the actions of the leader. Leaders are able to envision what *could be*, and this vision drives them. Managers, on the other hand, are interested in stating clearly what *is*. Their focus is on what actually *exists* now.

PASSION: The second quality of leaders is passion or energy. The Christian woman draws this energy from her passion to serve her Lord. Leaders seem to have a passion for whatever task they have undertaken. They bring a significant measure of their own energy to a project, and they release and direct the energies of others. Working with a real leader is renewing. A leader uses her own energy to replenish the energies of others, and remains uniquely able to tap previously unknown sources of energy.

COMMITMENT: A quality closely related to the first two is that of commitment. Commitment is easy to recognize, but difficult to describe. Commitment includes loyalty, but goes beyond. It encompasses the emotional, as well as the physical or intellectual pledge to support an idea or project. The stick-to-itiveness of leaders, their perseverance over time, and persistence in the face of enormous difficulties, are well noted. Endurance is not a burden for a leader. Her focus on the vision God has given her and her energy for the work needed to make that vision a reality provide strength and endurance. Her desire to be obedient to God's will keeps her on course.

RISK-TAKING: A fourth quality of leaders is risk-taking. Driven by their goals, leaders may not see the actions they take as being risky. They make decisions based on their intuitive sense of what must be done to make progress toward the goal. To those who are unable to see the "big picture" or the ultimate vision, however, some of the decisions a leader makes may seem irrational or even foolhardy. But, within the context of this vision, all choices seem matter-of-fact and logical. Once the Christian woman has committed her life to God, her decisions come from his leading and she can move confidently forward.

The abilities of the leader are primarily those that enable others to contribute their best talents and energies. Leaders know how to coach others—rewarding them for each bit of progress and encouraging them to continue. Leaders know how to develop others—refining their skills and commending appropriate risk-taking. Leaders know how to support others—offering them emotional support, as well as other kinds of assistance that help everyone succeed.

These characteristics of leadership are not *male* or *female*. They are *effective*. Even so, they seem to embody many traits and skills that come more naturally to women than to men. Leadership is more closely akin to nurturing than to ruling; more like guiding than demanding; and more like serving than being served.

Leaders do not always lead from the top of the organization or from the front of the room. More commonly, leaders lead from behind or beside. They support, encourage, assist, and inspire others to contribute to their fullest capacity. Leaders lead when they help others. The helper-leader combines the qualities of selflessness with the qualities of vision, passion, commitment, and risk-taking to produce a message and a model of righteousness.

This view of leadership, as opposed to traditional management, frees women to contribute more of their talents to their churches. When women have a vision of what *might* be anywhere in God's world, whether it is in their homes, their businesses, or their churches, they can contribute and lead in accomplishing this vision. They are no longer constrained by the view that leading is equal to seeking positions of authority or power. Churches are then free to tap the gifts of all their members more directly, without violating doctrine or challenging tradition.

This view does not mean, however, that it can be "business as usual" for most churches. It means, instead, that those in positions of authority within churches must examine and re-examine their actions and their underlying beliefs and attitudes. Are they taking the same view of women that is demonstrated in the Scriptures? Are they consciously seeking to open up opportunities for women to be able to contribute their full range of gifts within the church, even when this feels uncomfortable because "we've never done it this way before"? Even those with the most admirable intentions will be hard pressed to rid themselves of some less-than-useful attitudes and practices that have developed and become ingrained. For those in authority in our churches, adopting the position that all gifts within the congregation can and should be used for the glory of God is easier to say than it will be to live.

CHAPTER FOUR

The Arena

4

Glorify the LORD *with me: let us exalt his name together* (Psalm 34:3).

> Christ loved the church and gave himself up for her to make her holy, cleansing her by the washing with water through the word, and to present her to himself as a radiant church, without stain or wrinkle or any other blemish, but holy and blameless (Eph. 5:25b–27).

GOAL: To present the challenge to local churches to integrate the skills and abilities of *all* members into their ministries.

The church provides Christian women with a logical, viable context in which to express themselves as helper-leaders. The concept of a helper-leader certainly has implications for other segments of a woman's life, but the design of this book is to consider how this concept impacts ministry-opportunities for women within the church.

Many women love the church because they know that Christ pledged himself as the Bridegroom to the church. They feel compelled to operate within the context of a local

45

fellowship of believers. Women who have this view of the church want to function under the authority of the ordained leadership of the church. They do not want to be involved only in parachurch ministries. This is not to say that parachurch activities are wrong, but it is saying that parachurch ministries are not enough for many women. As one young woman expressed it, "I want to be involved in significant ministry within my church. It is the church that nurtured me as a child. It is the church where I was baptized. It is the church where I identified myself with Christ and attached myself to a particular group of believers. I want to serve the King within the context of his church. I want to employ the gifts he has given me for the advancement of his church." These are good and appropriate desires.

The practicing of spiritual gifts is God's plan for his church. Every gift is needed and every gift is valuable. Spiritual gifts are not given for private use. In 1 Corinthians 12, Paul instructs us on the use of spiritual gifts. He clearly states that these gifts are gifts of the Holy Spirit to individuals and are to be used "for the common good" (v. 7) of the church. He refutes the idea that some spiritual gifts are more valuable than others. Since the Giver of the gifts is the sole Determiner of both what the gift will be and who the recipient will be, it would be foolish for anyone else to attach degrees of value to the gifts. And Paul tells us, "I do not want you to be ignorant" (v. 1).

Paul uses a metaphor to explain the function of gifts in the church. The formation of the physical body required a creative act of God. He determined what the parts would be, how they would be arranged, and what their function would be. It is God who "arranged the parts in the body, every one of them, just as he wanted them to be" (1 Cor. 12:18). So it is with the church. Each local church is as much a creative act of God as is each body. God sovereignly arranges the "mix" according to his divine plan. He has determined which person has which gift(s). No gift is more important than any other. Your gift fits. Your gift is needed. God does not waste his creative acts. Isn't it interesting that the gifts are not divided into male and female lists? It is also interesting that one of the gifts is that of being "able to help others" (v. 28). Our privilege and responsibility is to demonstrate our obedience to the Giver of our gifts by discovering and developing them for the common good of the body. This is not just any body—this is the Body of Christ! What more fitting context for service to our Lord can there be?

The need for Christian women who are willing to minister as helper-leaders in their churches is incredible. Consider two other "helper" verses.

> The victim commits himself to you; you are the helper of the fatherless. (Ps. 10:14)

> For he will deliver the needy who cry out, the afflicted who have no one to help. (Ps. 72:12)

These verses open vivid vistas of opportunity for women who desire to imitate the Divine Helper by giving assistance to the victims, the fatherless, the needy, and the afflicted. Surely contemplating the implications of this compels us to move beyond confusion about our role to concern about the needs before us.

Urban Mission, a publication of Westminster Theological Seminary, stated in its May 1989 issue,

> The roles of women in urban ministry are enhanced by global urbanization. Some urban neighborhoods or people groups are so trapped in violence and despair that they can only be, if not best be, reached by women. We remember that the Aucas of Ecuador killed the men but later received the women and children who came. Some urban areas are so dangerous that they will probably only be reached by women. From Chicago to Calcutta, there are communities where women have organized and reached out uniquely from the powerless to the powerful. Only by mobilizing the whole church to take the whole gospel to the whole world will we effectively reach the whole world with the gospel. The vulnerability of the women becomes their power in urban ministry.

The task is too overwhelming and intimidating for most of us to tackle alone, but we have not been called to function

47

alone. The church is a body and is most effective when the various parts are working in harmony. So the next step in becoming actively concerned about the needs around us is to see how women in local churches can organize and mobilize to serve collectively as helper-leaders.

THE VALUE OF AN ORGANIZED WOMEN'S MINISTRY IN THE LOCAL CHURCH

Recently I (Susan) was in Washington participating in a Women's Leadership Task Force on Pornography. This was a highly emotional experience. As I became more and more aware of the enormity and vileness of this evil that threatens the moral fiber of our culture, I wanted to get up and run out of the room. I longed to be back in the safety of my own home. Then I looked at the picture of my grandson that I keep in my notebook. As I looked at his precious face I knew I had to stay in that room. I realized the need to do what I could for all the children who are growing up in a society that has made freedom of speech an idol.

I returned home determined to do something to make a difference. For days I prayed, "Father, what can I do? The problem is so big and I am so small. I have no idea where to begin." Then the Lord pressed a thought upon my heart, "You can't do everything, but you can do something. You can begin by being actively concerned about the children and youth in your own church. You can pray for their protection from this evil."

As I began to consider the number of children and teens in my church, even this task seemed overwhelming. My prayer would be little more than a "blanket" prayer. Then I remembered that I was not alone. There were twenty-five women in our weekly Bible study. Working together, we could "pray through" the list of children and teens much more effectively than I could ever have done alone. When I explained the issue, these women shared my burden. Together we developed a plan. Each week every woman draws the name of one child and commits to pray daily for God's protective covering over that

48

child. Each then writes a note of love and encouragement to the child she is praying for. Think of it! Twenty-five children are prayed for individually every week, and yet the task is doable for even the busiest woman.

In many churches, women have dropped out of the women's ministry because it simply does not meet their real needs nor does it offer opportunities for significant ministry. Most Christian women have multiple responsibilities and must make choices about how they will use their time, energies, and abilities. It is simply not good stewardship to attend boring, irrelevant meetings! However, a vital ministry can alleviate much confusion and frustration and direct women's gifts and experiences toward significant service.

The first steps in designing a women's ministry are to state the value and lay the foundation of such a ministry. Here we will list five of the many possible benefits of an organized women's ministry.

FIVE BENEFITS OF WOMEN'S MINISTRIES IN THE LOCAL CHURCH

A Framework for Growth and Ministry Within the Context of the Church

Many excellent independent Bible studies exist for women. These serve a real need. However, since they are designed to appeal to a broad doctrinal base they do not afford the opportunity to develop a deeper understanding of the theological distinctiveness of a particular church. Neither do independent Bible studies provide a channel for ministry within the church. A women's ministry provides a place for women to grow and serve within the doctrinal standards and under the authority of their own church. Women today must be theologically astute in order not to succumb to the subtle new-age, pop-culture philosophies that bombard us. Growing and serving under the authority of ordained leadership provide an important protection for women.

49

A Vehicle for Women To Develop and Exercise Leadership Skills

Mobilizing the energies and abilities of women requires all types of leadership skills. A women's ministry that is actively addressing the needs of women in various seasons and circumstances of life can use the full range of women's abilities and experiences and provide significant opportunities for every woman to develop and exercise her gifts and life-experiences.

A Means To Unify the Ministry of Women

The great variety of interests that women have, and the number of situations in which women find themselves, often contribute to a fragmented women's ministry. Older and younger women, married and single women, women who are one parent in a two-parent family and those who are single-parents, women who are able to remain at home and those who by choice or circumstances are employed outside the home, women who homeschool and those with children in either Christian or public schools, those who are activists politically or socially and those who aren't are all part of the church and in need of ministry outlets. Bringing unity out of such diversity seems impossible. The lack of communal bonds and support among women is painful for many. Women often feel isolated and alone.

A flexible, diversified women's ministry that encompasses all of the needs and interests of the women in a particular church can provide cohesiveness and support that transcends their different situations. It cannot be a narrow, one-track ministry that causes women to feel they must attend certain meetings or be involved in certain activities to be accepted. The ministry must have a broad scope—there must be many tracks so that each woman can select the one that is right for her and yet still feel that she is a part of the whole.

For example, a single mother who is employed outside the home may feel that she cannot leave her children to attend a women's Bible study. Thus she feels deprived of opportunities to establish meaningful relationships with other women. A creative women's ministry could meet this need by offering her the opportunity to be assigned to a ministry group comprised of, for example, another single mother and two widows. This group, including the children, could meet one Sunday afternoon a month for lunch and then visit shut-ins or a local nursing home. They would then be involved in meaningful ministry and still be able to form supportive relational bonds with other women. The single-parent women would not have to leave their children, and they would feel part of the total ministry of the church.

Another example: Women who are involved in a crisis pregnancy center may have no emotional or physical energy left to be involved in a ministry group or a Bible-study group. Thus they may feel isolated from the rest of the women in their church. In their isolation, they may falsely conclude that the other women do not support their efforts. A "community concerns" committee that would meet to pray not only about current social issues but also for those women who are actively involved would go a long way toward lessening the feeling of isolation. The socially involved women could channel their prayer requests to this group and an atmosphere of mutual support and encouragement would evolve. There may even be older women—even bedridden, or housebound women—who are physically unable to participate in pro-life activities but who want to pray specifically for the women who are on the front lines of this battle. Again this would give a sense of oneness and support to a number of women in different situations.

This blending of needs, interest, and abilities does not just happen. There must be an organized effort to bring all of these options under the umbrella of the women's ministry and to enlist women to participate. A well-crafted women's ministry provides a unity of purpose and connects women of diverse situations and interests, enabling them to join together in service and spiritual growth through the church.

A Vehicle for Women To Support the Total Ministry of the Church

A women's ministry is a vehicle to integrate the ministry of women and the total ministry of the church. One way to accomplish this is to have the officers of the women's ministry serve on the corresponding church committees. For example, if the woman who is missions chairperson for the women's ministry serves on the church missions committee, there is a clear channel of communication that involves women in supporting the church's missions program. When a women's ministry has systems in place to respond to needs, women can efficiently and effectively help the pastor when there is a crisis. For example, when there is a death, a pastor needs only a single contact to arrange meals for the family. An organized women's ministry makes it possible for women to collectively infuse a congregation with loving support and encouragement.

A Safe Place for Women To Cultivate Nurturing Relationships

One of our greatest strengths as women is our capacity to attach ourselves to another person—to nurture and to be nurtured. A women's ministry that recognizes this and provides opportunities for women to study, pray, and serve together, as well as opportunities to laugh and cry together, supplies that sense of acceptance and belonging that women need. It can also provide a context for obedience to the Titus 2 command.

> Likewise, teach the older women to be reverent in the way they live, not to be slanderers or addicted to much wine, but to teach what is good. Then they can train the younger women to love their husbands and children, to be self-controlled and pure, to be busy at home, to be kind, and to be subject to their husbands, so that no one will malign the word of God. (Titus 2:3-5)

One of the richest resources for developing helper-leaders are older women who have faithfully served the Lord through his church. They are credible role models. Their life-experi-

52

ences have given them a wisdom that can only come by living obediently through various seasons and situations of life. The need for these godly role models intensifies as more and more Christian young women do not live close to family and/or do not have Christian mothers. Within the local church, women of similar theological persuasions can be spiritually mothered and can also become spiritual mothers.

As women experience acceptance among other women, an environment is created where they are nurtured. Then they can identify and focus their gifts, interests, and energies on tasks that need to be undertaken for the advancement of the kingdom—and for the glory of our Sovereign King. This safe environment is also a place for non-Christian women to hear the gospel message in the context of love.

A women's ministry is not an end in itself. It is a tool to minister to the female population in a church and to mobilize them to serve as helper-leaders in the church. Other resources are available to help you develop a women's ministry.* Here we will only share some brief ideas on how to begin formulating or strengthening the organized women's ministry in your church.

THE FOUNDATION OF WOMEN'S MINISTRIES IN THE LOCAL CHURCH

Prayer

Those responsible for planning the women's ministry should spend time in prayer. Pray individually and corporately for God's leading. His glory should be the ultimate objective of the ministry. Pray for every woman in your church and for sensitivity to minister to her needs.

---

*One resource to help develop a women's ministry is *Loving Leadership: A Training Manual for Women In the Church* by Susan Hunt. This was written specifically for women in the Presbyterian Church in America, but is applicable to any women's ministry. It can be ordered from the PCA's Christian Education Bookstore: 1852 Century Place, Atlanta, Georgia 30345; 1-800-283-1357.

Vision

Develop a group vision of what that ministry needs to be by surveying all the women in your church and assessing needs and interests. It is important to gather data from women who are not involved so that you can broaden the scope of the ministry to include them. Also ask the male leadership of the church for their input. It is important to know what they need and expect from the ministry.

Goals

The leaders of the women's ministry should use the data gathered from the women and the male leadership to set goals for the ministry. Though the various goals may later be assigned to different women, the group should collectively adopt them so that everyone feels ownership of the total ministry. Once the goals are specified, the officers should plan a strategy to implement the goals, determine who will be responsible for each event and how each will happen, and plan programs and ministries for the year and schedule these events on the calendar.

Communication

Communicate the vision and the plans to all of the women in the church. Clear, repeated communication is vital to a successful ministry. It is important for the women to know that you listened to their ideas. People are more anxious to take part in something when they have had input.

Evaluation

Continually evaluate the ministry. Are you meeting real needs? Are objectives of each program being realized? If it's working don't fix it, but if it's not working do something!

PART TWO

THE ELEMENTS OF LEADERSHIP

We have developed the concept of the helper-leader and discussed the value of women serving within the context of the church. But how does the individual woman make the transfer from a concern in her heart to appropriate ministry in the church? How does the women's ministry in a church provide a meaningful context for women to serve as helper-leaders? How does the male leadership of the local church encourage the mobilization of its female members? We pray that the following life examples will help you to put the helper-leader principle into practice.

These life example emphasize focus, wisdom, confidence, and unity and they will be treated in separate chapters in this part. Our rationale is that focus on God develops wisdom that produces confidence to serve others and builds unity in God's church. This is a description of a helper-leader.

As you read the life examples introducing each chapter, you may think, "I know her," or, "That's me!" Keep in mind that these examples reflect real issues and situations, but they are not actual events that happened to a single person.

For many women, being a helper probably comes more

naturally than being a leader. There is something instinctive and there are cultural factors that cause us to know how to help others. Even though we need to continue refining this gift, we need to focus also on developing leadership skills. Some would suggest that to overtly work at being a leader is presumptuous and that such skills smack of manipulation. We contend that if we are going to function as helper-leaders in the church, we have a responsibility to increase our competency as leaders. Each of the following chapters concludes with a section on leadership skills. Our prayer is that these techniques will be tools to increase your ability to "lead many to righteousness."

CHAPTER FIVE

Focus

5

Glorify the LORD with me: let us exalt his name together (Psalm 34:3).

My eyes are ever on the LORD, for only he will release my feet from the snare (Ps. 25:15).

GOAL: To help women recognize the freedom from confusion that comes in living out their primary purpose—to glorify God.
To illustrate the qualities of a helper-leader from the life of Priscilla.

LIFE EXAMPLE

Let's return to our example from chapter one.

"I have to admit that I leave meetings like this feeling frustrated and not really appreciated. I feel put down by a group of men who seem to be patting me on the head and saying,

'We'll take over now.'" Christy was cautiously revealing her annoyance, and I had to admit that I could understand her feelings. She had worked so long to raise the consciousness of members of her church to a particular need. At first, no one seemed to share her burden. Then the issue became a "hot item" and suddenly everyone was concerned. The male leadership of the church became involved and organized a meeting to decide how to meet the need. Christy was given a few minutes on the agenda, but the men were clearly the "movers and shakers."

If you asked Christy, she would tell you that she usually has no problems with the traditional biblical interpretation of male headship. But somehow, at times like this when the idea of headship is put into practice, traditional views of headship just do not "fit" for her. The elders of the church were the only ones in the position to make decisions; yet if you had added up their collective knowledge on this issue, it would not even have begun to approach Christy's expertise.

"This issue is a big one to me," Christy lamented, "My heart is in it, and I've been gathering information and working on it for more than a year! They asked me to give them some background on the issue. They also suggested that, since I was concerned about making sure things went smoothly for the meeting, I take charge of the nursery and fellowship time. Then what do they do? The meeting ended with three elders being appointed to do more study."

Christy's delight that something was being done was overshadowed by a growing resentment over who was in charge and a growing suspicion that the issue would remain "in committee" for months. Her expertise in this area was apparently being unacknowledged and unappreciated, and she was confused and hurt.

Have you ever felt this way?

LESSONS FROM SCRIPTURE

Perhaps a look at the helper qualities of availability, adaptability, anticipation, and ability in Priscilla's life will give us some clues about dealing with a situation such as Christy's. When we examine her reactions to the events in her life it seems that she must have been a woman who had joyfully embraced God's glory and was energetically and creatively living out this reason for being. Her roles, abilities, circumstances, and opportunities were as varied as any woman of today. These factors in her life were constantly changing. But it seems that the central fact of her life, her commitment to glorify God and to enjoy him, was unchangeable. This unchangeable factor enabled her to exhibit the qualities of a helper. Paul's missionary effort is the main plot being developed in Acts 18, but an intriguing subplot is the ministry of the husband-and-wife team of Aquila and Priscilla. A character study of Priscilla provides a portrait of a helper.

> After this, Paul left Athens and went to Corinth. There he met a Jew named Aquila, a native of Pontus who had recently come from Italy with his wife Priscilla, because Claudius had ordered all the Jews to leave Rome. Paul went to see them, and because he was a tentmaker as they were, he stayed and worked with them. . . . So Paul stayed for a year and a half. . . . (Acts 18:1–3, 11)

Priscilla and Aquila had only recently arrived in Corinth. It is likely that Priscilla had not unpacked the boxes nor found drapes for the guest room, yet her home was available to this itinerant preacher—not just for two or three nights but for a year and a half!

Here Priscilla displays "Helper Quality #1."

Availability

Priscilla was willing to extend the ministry of hospitality. There was no complaining, "I am so stressed-out with this forced move . . . having to leave my friends and even my fine china behind . . . I can't possibly entertain a guest now." There were no excuses, "But hospitality is not my spiritual gift—my gift is teaching."

Could it be that Priscilla was simply available to do what needed to be done because her objective was to glorify God?

Housing Paul for such a long period of time must have been a decision made by both Aquila and Priscilla. If Paul's presence in their home had caused any friction in their marriage, Paul would never have stayed. Perhaps it was during this time that Aquila and Priscilla caught Paul's vision. They were increasingly willing to give assistance and support—even though that assistance and support involved the unglamorous tasks of feeding and caring for a visitor in their home, because they were advancing toward the same objective.

Availability prepared the way for the development of "Helper Quality #2."

Adaptability

"Paul stayed on in Corinth for some time. Then he left the brothers and sailed for Syria, accompanied by Priscilla and Aquila" (Acts 18:18). For most women, there is some degree of trauma involved in moving. No matter what excitement the new destination holds, tearing away from the present situation is heart-rending. Priscilla and Aquila were *forced* by Claudius to leave Rome, but a year and a half later they *chose* to accompany Paul to Ephesus. We marvel at this woman, who was probably still trying to "find those drapes for the guest room," being willing to uproot and move on! Priscilla's willingness to adapt put her in a position to be a helper to her husband and to Paul. They were not hindered by what could have been a reluctance to move but rather were encouraged by her full participation in this missionary enterprise.

> They arrived at Ephesus, where Paul left Priscilla and Aquila. . . . Meanwhile a Jew named Apollos, a native of Alexandria, came to Ephesus. He was a learned man, with a thorough knowledge of the Scriptures. He had been instructed in the way of the Lord, and he spoke with great fervor and taught about Jesus accurately, though he knew only the

baptism of John. He began to speak boldly in the synagogue. When Priscilla and Aquila heard him, they invited him to their home and explained to him the way of God more adequately. (Acts 18:19, 24–26)

In this passage we see "Helper Quality #3."

Anticipation

When Apollos arrived in Ephesus, Priscilla and Aquila realized his potential and accurately assessed his weakness. Apollos was an articulate speaker with a thorough knowledge of the Scriptures—to a point. As they listened to this mighty preacher, Aquila and Priscilla realized that he had not been adequately educated as to the work and ministry of Jesus. Apollos was unaware that he was leaving crucial elements of doctrine out of his preaching. But, Aquila and Priscilla were able to help Apollos convert a weakness into a strength.

Many times the person who needs help does not even realize it. A helper anticipates need and lovingly reaches out. Developing a quiet sense of anticipation of another's need, and the gentle sensitivity that enables one to come alongside in an unoffensive way, is characteristic of the ministry of help. The helper, whose objective is God's glory, is able to anticipate a need and to supply what is needed.

There is something else here that should not be missed: It is often easier to be free of self-promotion than another's promotion. Many times the tendency is to manipulate a situation in order to put someone else (perhaps a spouse or best friend) in the spotlight. We are impressed that Priscilla made no effort to promote Aquila. As women we should certainly be concerned about the success of others, but it should be appropriate concern that does not get in the way of focusing on God's glory. If Priscilla had promoted public glory for Aquila in this instance, she would have set the stage for competition between Aquila and Apollos. Priscilla's influence would then have been destructive rather than helpful.

Paul had enough confidence in Aquila and Priscilla to leave them in Ephesus. This confidence was confirmed in how they handled the situation with Apollos. Not only did they anticipate the need, but here we also see "Helper Quality #4."

Ability

Though they were tentmakers and not trained theologians, Aquila and Priscilla were intelligent Christians who had learned well from Paul. Their desire to glorify God, combined with a knowledge of the Word, produced a sound theology that was the basis of their ministry of helping. When they began their teaching, Apollos immediately recognized their competence in the Word as well as their ministry. Priscilla and Aquila were disciples who discipled.

Ability without humility, however, can become arrogance. All three people in this account displayed beautiful humility. We see Apollos' humility in his willingness to be taught by a tentmaker and his wife. We see the humility of Priscilla and Aquila in their willingness to remain in the background and receive no credit for their efforts. They were content for Apollos to preach publicly what they had taught him privately.

Priscilla and Aquila were not in a power struggle with Paul nor with Apollos because neither of them had a hidden agenda. There was no self-promotion. Instead they were all committed to the same objective—glorifying God. They did not value one person's ministry over another, so there was no competition. Priscilla and Aquila were content to help Paul and Apollos, and Paul lovingly acknowledged their supportive ministry in Romans 16:3-4, "Greet Priscilla and Aquila, my fellow workers in Christ Jesus. They risked their lives for me. Not only I but all the churches of the Gentiles are grateful to them."

The primary focus of these passages is really not Priscilla's character development. Yet perhaps there is a significant progression in her life that will help us transfer the principles of being a helper-leader into practice.

Priscilla's availability gave her the unique opportunity to be instructed by the apostle Paul. As she grew in her understanding of the gospel, it seems that Priscilla began to focus on the awesomeness of God's glory rather than the importance of her immediate circumstances.

Perhaps her adaptability did not come from a desire to move from place to place but from her commitment to glorify God. Her worldview grew to encompass more than her little world—it expanded to include God's sovereign plan for his world and her place in that plan.

Priscilla's availability and adaptability might well have given her an increased sensitivity to others. As she was "stretched" through her availability and through adapting to changes, the resulting maturity made her a woman who anticipated the needs of others. As we saw, Priscilla eventually had the opportunity to help instruct a man who became a leader in the church. When this opportunity came, she had the ability to meet the challenge, because she was prepared.

As we reflect on the example of Priscilla, it helps clarify our thinking about Christy's situation. If our focus is on anything other than God's glory, we will be as unsteady and fragmented as our roles, abilities, circumstances, and opportunities at any given moment. If our starting point is the glory of God, then these roles, abilities, circumstances, and opportunities become a means of fulfilling our purpose. We will not be distracted by who is doing what or by a time-frame imposed on us, because we are available to do whatever is necessary to accomplish our objective of glorifying God.

Christy's ultimate problem was not the men in her church. The real problem was her focus. "My eyes are ever on the LORD, for only he will release my feet from the snare" (Ps. 25:15). When our eyes are on the Lord we are free from the snare of self-centeredness, self-interest, and self-promotion. The hard truth is that as Christian women we must first confront these internal "self" problems that cloud our focus. When we are clear about our focus, the external pressures of the world shouting chauvinism, lack of acknowledgement and appreciation, relegation to domestic chores, and limited opportunities to use spiritual gifts will not easily distract us. We are then liberated to pour all our energies and creativity into glorifying God.

We do not mean to minimize the reality of these external pressures. The point is that these pressures are a snare that will entrap us. When we focus on the externals—the actions and attitudes of others, the culture, the "system," etc.—we erect barriers that hinder effective ministry. Only a clear focus on God's glory frees us to serve him as helper-leaders.

Priscilla apparently never sought position nor worried about whether her efforts were appreciated. Because of this, she helped Aquila, Paul, and Apollos fulfill their missions. The power of her quiet influence in the lives of these men—and thus in the life of the early church—cannot be underestimated. We wonder whether she even was aware of the power of her influence. Probably not, for concern about her influence would have distracted her from simply doing what needed to be done. Priscilla obviously was not confused over her role. She was concerned about God's glory.

Bright, qualified, caring women do face the frustration and hurt that Christy faced. We must see this as a subtle attempt of Satan to redirect our focus. Once our focus is on anything other than God's glory we are vulnerable to the enemy's attack.

It is not only women who are confronted with the problem of misdirected focus. Have you ever wondered about the struggle the King of the universe must have had in that upper room as he watched twelve men waiting for someone to come in and perform the domestic chore of washing their feet? Satan must have tried to take full advantage of that situation. "Only a few hours and you will be on a cross—you had better work through your feelings. Most of your efforts have been wasted on this bunch of lazy, unappreciative men. Why bother to teach another lesson? If you perform the foot-washing chore you will degrade the position of King—you must protect that position. Surely there is something more important to be done. Why not preach a sermon?"

But the Sovereign Lord became a Servant.

Your attitude should be the same as that of Christ Jesus:
Who, being in very nature God, did not consider equality
with God something to be grasped, but made himself

nothing, taking the very nature of a servant, being made in human likeness. And being found in appearance as a man, he humbled himself and became obedient to death—even death on a cross! Therefore God exalted him to the highest place and gave him the name that is above every name, that at the name of Jesus every knee should bow, in heaven and on earth and under the earth, and every tongue confess that Jesus Christ is Lord, to the glory of God the Father." (Phil. 2:5–11)

The Father is clearly pleased with and glorified by a servant spirit.

Let us now consider some practical ways to implement these concerns.

NEXT STEPS FOR CHRISTY

Christy's situation presents her with the opportunity to glorify God by being available to do whatever is needed. She may have to make an adjustment from being in charge to being in the background. If she tells the male leaders in her church how glad she is that they now share her concern, and if she lovingly and cheerfully helps in whatever way she is asked, she will demonstrate her willingness to supply what is needed to accomplish their shared goals. Christy must be careful to communicate a willingness to adapt to the plans and schedule of the men in the offices of authority. She must avoid showing a lack of trust or disappointment in their strategy. However, this does not mean she should remain passive. In addition to responding to their requests, it is appropriate for Christy to initiate some action.

She could become an active, knowledgeable prayer warrior for the committee. Her knowledge of the issue would enable her to prayerfully anticipate the needs of the elders of the church, perhaps even before they realize they have needs. Christy could organize some of her resource material, highlighting significant portions, and privately offer it to the chairman of the commit-tee. Remember, Priscilla and Aquila taught Apollos privately what he eventually preached publicly.

NEXT STEPS FOR MEN IN
OFFICES OF AUTHORITY

Elders in a church can rarely afford the luxury of putting a great amount of attention on any one issue. Wise and effective elders will therefore use the gifts and knowledge of all the members of the church as well as seek guidance from qualified research people before making a decision. The elders, then, could ask Christy to write a position paper or serve on a task force to study the issue, since many women like Christy, free from the time-consuming, administrative duties that confront elders, can focus their energy on one particular issue. Think of the effectiveness—the completeness—in a church that uses the gifts of women like Christy. Elders will make better decisions, women will experience more fulfillment, and the entire congregation will benefit.

STRATEGY FOR THE WOMEN'S MINISTRY

An effective women's ministry should be sensitive to the many social issues confronting us today and should provide avenues for appropriate Christian activism. Such a ministry will provide women like Christy a place in which to mobilize other women with similar concerns. It also provides a conduit to channel information to other women and to enlist their prayer support.

Another strategy is to have a mechanism in place that will allow women to voice their concerns and to bring their issue before the male leadership. An excellent way to do this is to have the chairpersons of the various women's committees serve on the corresponding committees for the church at large. These might include missions, worship, education, outreach, fellowship, etc. Too often there is no avenue of communication and women like Christy feel isolated and alone. Then they feel frustrated, confused, and hurt when something begins to happen without their having an opportunity to voice their position. A women's ministry that is functioning as a part of the total ministry of the church prevents this situation from happening.

LEADERSHIP SKILLS FOR WOMEN

Those who are wise will shine like the brightness of the heavens, and those who lead many to righteousness, like the stars for ever and ever. (Dan. 12:3)

A skill, according to our favorite definition, is "a learned power of doing something competently" (Webster's Ninth New Collegiate Dictionary). Leadership skills can be learned, and they certainly do bring a new sense of power and competence to the individual using them. Skills are like muscles; they grow and develop when we systematically exercise them. In this section we will introduce you to some skills that women need in order to use their gifts effectively. In order to develop these skills, you must find small, nonthreatening challenges with which to begin. As your leadership skills develop and become more a part of you, take on larger challenges.

The first three skills we will discuss are leadership skills that Christy needs to be able to call on—creativity, perseverance, and strategic thinking.

Creativity. Although some people are given specific gifts in creativity, everyone can learn to be more creative. Creativity is the ability to generate new ideas, methods, or processes. These can come from fresh approaches to combining old, familiar ideas, or they can come from fresh creations. If you are thinking, "that's just not me," we encourage you to think some more.

Most people limit their creativity with the negative messages they tell themselves. "I'm just not clever enough," or "If I were as talented as Rosemary, I wouldn't mind trying." We encourage you to replace these messages with positive questions, "What can I try that is even a little different from what I have been doing?" "How else can I describe the problem I am trying to solve?" Or, "Can I add a new twist to make it work better?"

Creativity comes when you open your thinking, or brainstorm. Try this simple exercise. Take a box of baking soda. Make a list of at least twenty different things (as silly as you want) that you could us this for, if you were not using it for its normal purposes. Limit yourself to three minutes. This same kind of brainstorming is useful in developing creative ideas for any dilemma you are facing. It works even better when two or three people work together: Then, you can build on each other's ideas. However, it is most important that you avoid judging ideas as they emerge. Get out as many ideas as you can, then go back and regroup them based on how likely you think they are to be sound approaches to solving your problem.

Another technique for developing your creativity is to think about it metaphorically. Again, this is a simple approach to help you address the problem from a different angle. For example, pretend that your problem or challenge is a lion. What can you do to tame this lion? You might train it (as lion tamers do), you might befriend it, or you might feed it. Do you get the point? Once you create a metaphor for your problem, the solutions also emerge as metaphors. The next step is to say, "Now how in real life do I accomplish these things?"

Perseverance. This second leadership skill is the ability to persist over time, never abandoning your cause and never taking actions that close doors that will eventually need to be opened if you are to accomplish your goals. One effective approach to the development of perseverance is to adopt the motto: *There are no failures, only new learnings.* When all the delays and apparent setbacks are seen as opportunities rather than discouragements your whole perspective changes.

Another way to build perseverance is to set up intermediate milestones. Establish small goals and reward yourself as you achieve them. Too often, we see only the final step of a project as the one worth celebrating.

A final approach is to establish a support network. Don't think that a support network has to be large. Even a small group of one or two supporters who are willing to pray specifically for you as you develop leadership skills, will be sufficient. Share your accomplishments—large and small. Listen to their ideas for getting through the difficulties.

Strategic thinking. A third skill area that every woman needs to develop is that of strategic thinking. It is so easy to miss the big picture when we focus so intently on only a small section of the picture that especially interests us. In order to develop strategic thinking abilities, try to develop a map of all the other programs or processes that relate to what you want to accomplish (including those that you believe conflict with your goal). Become the advocate for each of these in turn. Then, develop statements that expand your position. This will help you position your goals in the larger picture.

A second approach to developing strategic thinking is to do something we call "consequence analysis." This is the process by which you assume to take a certain course of action, and then project what you think are the most likely results of this action. After you have the most likely (first) results, project the second most likely outcomes, the third most likely, and so forth until you have exhausted your thinking on further possibilities. Also take into consideration all the other groups (or even individuals) who might be affected by what you want to do: Think through what will happen to them and how they are likely to feel about your actions. Strategic thinking will provide information that can guide you in involving others where appropriate and in making wiser choices that are more likely to be effective over the long run.

WHAT COULD BE

Consider the difference in the example at the beginning of this chapter and the following:

As Christy and I walked out of the meeting, her "cup was running over." Several months earlier God had burdened her heart for the unwed mothers of our community. Because of her concern about social issues, she was a member of the women's Salt and Light committee. This committee kept the women of the church informed so they could pray and become involved in

71

social issues to whatever degree they felt led. The chairperson of the women's committee was also a member of the church S & L committee.

The women had been involved in helping staff the local crisis pregnancy center, but Christy had begun to feel they should provide housing for unwed mothers who chose to have their babies. She shared her burden with the women's S & L committee and they began praying about it. After a creative brainstorming session, they developed a strategy based on a shared vision of success regarding this project. It was helpful for Christy to share with her sisters in Christ—she no longer felt alone and isolated. The concern was shared with the church S & L committee and they joined in praying for direction. After several weeks of prayer, the committee presented the housing need to the elders of the church. The elders then appointed a task force to study the issue. Christy was a member of that task force and she patiently worked with the members to help them move to the same level of concern she and the women's S & L committee were on. After much investigation and research, the task force brought a proposal to the elders. In turn the elders adopted the proposal and took it to the congregation.

No wonder Christy's cup was running over! At the meeting we had just left the congregation had voted to purchase a house for unwed mothers.

What a different story when male leadership in a church realizes the wisdom of putting systems into place that creatively employ the gifts of all of the members.

72

CHAPTER SIX

Wisdom

6

Glorify the LORD with me; let us exalt his name together (Psalm 34:3).

The fear of the LORD is the beginning of wisdom, and knowledge of the Holy One is understanding (Prov. 9:10).

GOAL: To explore external barriers that seem to restrict women from exercising their spiritual gifts in the context of a church that holds to the male headship position.

To stimulate men and women in these churches to think creatively about ways to break these barriers without violating the biblical position of male headship.

LIFE EXAMPLES

Lauren, an information systems manager in a major communications company, looked at me intently and said, "I don't understand it. . . . My spiritual gifts seem to be male gifts. I don't relate to the traditional things women do, and the women in my church certainly don't relate to the things I do. My training, gifts, and experiences are more in the areas of

75

organizing, directing, and supervising people; but there seems to be no place for women to use these abilities in the church. I often feel that my professional success is resented by the men in my church and is a threat to the women. It is especially difficult because I want and need the support of other Christian women. I tried attending some of the women's functions, but I felt out of place. Even my husband can't understand why I feel so unfulfilled in the church. I am not sure I am in agreement with our church's position on the role of women, but I love this church. I am sure it is the best place for our family, and because of this I have placed myself under the authority of the governing body of the church. It is an issue of integrity for me that I should not oppose a position that I was aware of when I joined this church, but my frustration sometimes makes me appear adversarial. I just want to feel like a valued, contributing member, and there seems to be no place for me. Is there no way that my gifts and experiences can be utilized to serve?"

Anne graduated from seminary with a master's degree in Christian education. She is married and is not employed outside her home. She is a high-energy woman with a deep love for the Lord and the doctrinal position of her church, and she wants to use her training within her church. The Christian education committee in her church has had little focus or direction. This has been reflected in the types of educational programs that have been offered. Anne has heard other members discuss their wishes for more creativity in the educational programs. Recently, the chairperson of the committee resigned. Anne took this opportunity to write a proposal, including the approach she would take to reorganize the educational program, and to volunteer to serve as chairperson of the committee. The officers in her church (all male) responded saying that they agreed with the direction she had proposed for the educational programs, but that it would not be appropriate for a woman to head a church committee. When Anne heard this, she was very hurt. She believes that the elders in the church misunderstood her intent and interpreted her offer as being aggressive. She is also frustrated because Christian education is her field and she is not allowed to use her training in her own church where there is such a need—just because she is a woman! "I have to admit," said Anne, "that right now I am so angry I feel like just leaving this church and going to one that will appreciate my gifts and my desire to serve, but I am confused. I understand and support the biblical doctrine of male headship in the church. I also believe that God has called and prepared me for a special work. What am I supposed to do?"

Both of these women are experiencing the reality of the tension between accepting the position of male headship in the church and exercising their gifts for the good of the church. The most obvious choices for Lauren and Anne might seem to be to stand their ground and fight for the opportunity to use their gifts, even if this led to dissension and divisiveness, or to leave their churches for other, more liberal congregations where they might more easily use their gifts. These fight-or-flight choices may seem to be the only options, but surely our Creator is not limited only to these choices. Can this kind of conflict become a win-win situation for women like Lauren and Anne and for the church? We think so—in fact we have poured enormous energy into this book because we believe so intensely about this very issue.

Proverbs 14:1 says, "The wise woman builds her house, but with her own hands the foolish one tears hers down." There are many women like Lauren and Anne who have no desire to fragment the unity in their churches. They are not trying to change the structure of male headship. Their struggle comes in knowing how to handle the tension of submitting to authority and using their gifts for the common good of the church. In these kinds of situations, to build unity, rather than destroy it, requires enormous wisdom and discipline.

LESSONS FROM SCRIPTURE

There is a woman in Scripture who must have experienced some of the same kinds of conflicts that women like Lauren and Anne feel. She must have felt out of place, and she was certainly misunderstood by another woman, by her husband, and by the male leader in her church. Yet she did not succumb to the fight-or-flight mind-set.

First Samuel 1 gives the account of Hannah—a woman who had a positive influence in the kingdom even though she was surrounded by potentially explosive situations in her life. By refusing to take either the fight or the flight approaches, Hannah's life provides us with a model of a wise, disciplined woman whose actions and reactions displayed grace in the midst of agitating circumstances. Her life shows us that there is another way—the way of prayerful waiting. (*Please* don't close this book thinking that this is just another women-must-be-submissively-silent approach. Give us a chance to develop the concept of prayerful waiting as a creative, logical action plan for those desiring change.)

Hannah suffered the pain of infertility in a culture that intensified her misery and in a home where there was another wife who had children and who flaunted the fact before Hannah. Scripture tells us that this "rival kept provoking her in order to irritate her" (I Sam. 1:6).

Why would Peninnah, the other wife, have done such a cruel thing? We learn from the passage that Elkanah, the husband in this threesome, loved Hannah more. Is it any wonder that there was tension and conflict between these two women? Quite likely, Peninnah was making an all-out attempt to discredit Hannah. If she could evoke a reaction of rage, then she could tell Elkanah that Hannah was behaving unkindly toward her and perhaps gain his favor.

It is interesting that Scripture records no verbal response

from Hannah. Her weeping and her inability to eat indicate the depth of her hurt and sorrow, but apparently she did not fight back or defend herself. There was no attempt on Hannah's part to subtly oppose the situation by manipulating Elkanah to make a choice—neither did she threaten to leave home if he did not change these unfavorable conditions!

Perhaps Hannah understood the real source of Peninnah's bitter spirit toward her—insecurity. After all, Elkanah had made no secret of the fact that Hannah was his first love, even though she had no children. Hannah exercised a disciplined restraint by refusing to be a destructive influence. Instead, Hannah silently endured the insults and did not flaunt the fact that she was the favorite. In some situations conflict must be confronted. At other times the discipline of silence is a beautiful display of God's grace that builds rather than disrupts unity in his church.

The proverbs of Solomon were written that we might attain "wisdom and discipline" (Prov. 1:2). Consider the discipline involved in these proverbs.

> Starting a quarrel is like breaching a dam; so drop the matter before a dispute breaks out. (Prov. 17:14)
>
> Do not say, "I'll pay you back for this wrong!" Wait for the LORD, and he will deliver you. (Prov. 20:22)

Waiting on the Lord is not a passive act as is waiting for a storm to pass. This waiting is active as in waiting on or serving guests sitting at your dinner table. It is active because it requires serving our Father by focusing on his power to deliver us, and trusting him to make or not make changes in our situations.

Then, as if the energy expended on handling the other wife were not enough, Hannah's husband also became a potential source of her frustration and hurt. His response to her pain lacked sensitivity to say the least! Elkanah's query, "Don't I mean more to you than ten sons?" is not the issue. Hannah's heart was breaking and she needed sympathy. Not only did he fail to understand her sense of unfulfillment, but his answer probably added pressure to her already stressful situation.

Again we see Hannah graciously restraining herself. There is no evidence that she allowed self-pity to gain control or that she became immobilized by her pain. Hannah knew that Elkanah was not her enemy—he loved her. She understood that even though his remark was insensitive, his motive was concern. Men are often solution-oriented; women are often feeling-oriented. One is not better than the other—just different. The wise woman realizes her tendency to have strong feelings and appreciates the balance of the male tendency to consider solutions before feelings. Rather than reacting against Elkanah, Hannah wisely listened and avoided strife.

> It is to a man's honor to avoid strife, but every fool is quick to quarrel. (Prov. 20:3)

Hannah did not resort to fight or flight, but neither did she retreat. She went to the Lord in prayer. Prayerful waiting on the Lord is creatively active. It means opening ourselves to the most powerful Change-Agent in the universe!

Even as Hannah was in the temple in Shiloh praying, we see that there was a third relationship with the potential for conflict. Her fellowship with the Lord was so deep that she was apparently oblivious to anyone else being around. "In bitterness of soul Hannah wept much and prayed to the LORD. . . . Hannah was praying in her heart, and her lips were moving but her voice was not heard" (1 Sam. 1:10, 13). Eli, the priest, watching her, thought she was drunk. He added two and two together and came up with five. He approached her, and without asking the obvious, "Can I help?" accused her. "How long will you keep on getting drunk? Get rid of your wine" (1 Sam. 1:14).

Can you imagine how his words must have cut into her already troubled heart? She must have expected to find comfort from the man of God, but instead she received rebuke! Once again Hannah wisely restrained herself from reacting in anger to Eli's harsh words. What an uproar she would have caused if she had run out of the temple and told her family and friends about

Eli's false accusation. The battle lines would have been drawn—those for Eli and those for Hannah. Confusion would have ensued as each party retold the episode. Instead, Hannah exercised discipline and overlooked the offense.

A man's wisdom gives him patience; it is to his glory to overlook an offense. (Prov. 19:11)

Hannah overlooked the offense, but she did not remain silent. No useful purpose would have been served in responding to the other wife or to Elkanah. However, in this situation, a calm, clarification of the facts was in order. Hannah had been offended. . .Eli was operating on the basis of wrong information. . .the issue needed to be resolved. But she did not attack Eli—he was not her enemy, though it could have been interpreted that way at that moment. She overlooked the offense, addressed the issue, and received a blessing.

A gentle answer turns away wrath, but a harsh word stirs up anger. (Prov. 15:1)

Hannah gently explained her situation to Eli, avoiding any words of accusation. To Eli's credit he did not become defensive of his actions but lovingly replied, "Go in peace, and may the God of Israel grant you what you have asked of him" (1 Sam. 1:17).

Not only did Hannah make a friend of a potential enemy, but her wise course of action created a win-win situation for herself and for Eli. The result was that Eli became her advocate. He interceded on Hannah's behalf before the Lord and the change she longed for was accomplished—Hannah's barrenness was changed to fruitfulness! Prayerful waiting was surely the most logical, positive plan of action this woman could have followed.

We are captivated by Hannah. She was not a cold, unfeeling woman who was indifferent to the abuse, insensitivity, and misunderstanding she suffered. Hannah was a gentle woman with tender feelings. How could such tenderness be combined with calculated discipline? Often a woman with control appears harsh, and a woman with tender emotions seems to lack the fortitude needed to be a leader. Yet the blending of the knowledge *of* God and obedience *to* God is the essence of wisdom. It seems to us that Hannah's wisdom came from her focus. Hannah's knowledge of the character of God was her focal point. The powerful principle that governed her actions and reactions was obedience. She demonstrated this obedience through prayer and patience.

In the remaining verses of 1 Samuel 1 we see that Hannah bore a son. When the child was weaned she took him to live in the temple in Shiloh in obedience to the vow she had made to the Lord. Her determination to serve within the context of the church, even though she had suffered misunderstanding in the church, and though it was known throughout Israel that Eli's sons were practicing wickedness in the temple, is another evidence of her obedience. When she stood before Eli, she reminded him that she was the woman he had seen praying. Isn't it typical of Hannah that she did not mention the negative part of that encounter! We see no evidence of bitterness or anger on her part; just joy in being able to keep her vow to the Lord. "I prayed for this child, and the LORD has granted me what I asked of him. So now I give him to the LORD. For his whole life he will be given over to the LORD" (vv. 27–28).

Then Hannah prayed.

This prayer, recorded in 1 Samuel 2, gives us the clue to the source of Hannah's wisdom. The prayer begins, "My heart rejoices in the LORD. . ." She continues by praising God for his attributes of holiness, knowledge, justice, and compassion. Throughout the prayer we see her reliance on the sovereignty of God. It is interesting that this is not a prayer of thanksgiving for the gift of a son, but it is a prayer of praise for the Giver of the gift. Our impression is that Hannah would have prayed this prayer even if she had not received her heart's desire, for the focus of the prayer is the character of God. Hannah's fear of the Lord, her knowledge of the Holy One was the source of her wisdom.

Hannah was not ruled by her circumstances. She focused

on kingdom thinking and on God's glory rather than on her own situation. Therefore, Hannah could combine gentleness and discipline in a way that minimized conflict and maximized unity. Even while suffering the pain of infertility in the context of difficult relationships, her focus was so firmly fixed on Jehovah that she could live a life of obedience. She did not sink into a sea of self-pity, anger, or bitterness. She did not fight the situation or flee from it. She was a wise woman whose life made a positive statement for the kingdom.

The ability to stay focused is a wonderful skill. The story of Peter stepping out of the boat into the storm-tossed sea and walking on the water to meet Jesus illustrates the importance of staying focused on Jesus. As long as Peter's gaze was focused, he actually walked on top of the water. We don't know of another person who has ever lived on this planet who has taken even one step on top of the water—at least Peter wasn't with the rest of the disciples sitting in the boat just watching! But we also know that if Peter had stayed focused, he would not have encountered trouble. Some would criticize Peter for looking down at the waves lapping around his ankles, but we love and admire him. To his credit, when he did look down and saw that he was beginning to sink, he knew where to look for help. He was not foolish enough to try to swim back to the boat in that turbulent water. He looked to Jesus, took his strong hand, and together the two of them walked back to the boat.

As women there are times when our circumstances are turbulent. Some people tell us to leave the current circumstances for more favorable circumstances. Some tell us to change our circumstances. Some tell us that we must change ourselves—focus on our own needs and desires since we *cannot* change our circumstances.

The confusion in all of this is that there may be times when, humanly, all of these options make sense to us. But the bottom line is that if we are focused on God's love and his sovereignty, our lives will come into focus. There will be a distinctness and clarity most rare in this day of confusion. Rather than sinking into the circumstances of life, we will actually be able to take steps of faith on top of the circumstances. Focusing on Jesus will enable us to embrace his promise that ". . .in all things God works for the good of those who love him, who have been called according to his purpose. For those God foreknew he also predestined to be conformed to the likeness of his Son. . ." (Rom. 8:28–29).

As Christians, we are a people in process; and in God's economy the process is more important than the program *we* desire to see implemented or the change *we* desire to see occur. Sanctification is defined in the Westminster Shorter Catechism as ". . .the work of God's free grace, whereby we are renewed in the whole man after the image of God, and are enabled more and more to die unto sin, and live unto righteousness." (WSC, Q. 35) Our sanctification, our being conformed to the image of Jesus, is our Father's goal for us. Over and over in his Word he tells us that often it is through adverse circumstances that the Holy Spirit brings about internal, sanctifying changes in our hearts.

Hannah's wisdom, obedience, and focus would not have developed so beautifully nor sparkled so brilliantly without the pain and frustrations she endured. If Hannah had given birth to Samuel, and if he had served the Lord without her having to go through a waiting period of emotional suffering, we would still have had the marvelous stories about this obedient man, but we would have been deprived of Hannah's story because there would not have been a story.

If our focus is on God's sovereign love, and we are clinging to his promise to work all things together in such a way as to conform us to the image of Jesus, then we will have the wisdom to view situations such as Lauren and Anne faced not as attempts to stifle our gifts, but as opportunities to stimulate our sanctification. But again, prayerful waiting is not passive. As in the case of Hannah, there are times when prayerful waiting should manifest itself in wise clarification of intentions. So what could be done to create a win-win situation for women like Lauren and Anne and for the church?

NEXT STEPS FOR LAUREN AND ANNE

The church is not always the easiest place in which to serve. Perhaps the wise course of action for women like Lauren and Anne is to actively wait on the Lord, pouring more energy into focusing on Jesus and praying, as Hannah did. Hannah did not attack or accuse those around her about the injustices she suffered. She took her problems to the Lord. The first step for both Lauren and Anne, then, is to spend significant time in prayer, listening to the Lord, pouring out their hearts, and asking for wisdom. When they are able to move from a position of "I want to do this," to one that asks, "Lord, what do you want to have happen through me?" they will be ready to move ahead.

The second step for each of them is to discuss her situation with an officer in the church whom they personally respect. This may be risky. If these women want to exercise their leadership abilities, however, they must be willing to take risks when it is appropriate. Before this conversation, they must be sure that they have resolved any jealousy, anger, or other unhealthy motives and be ready to listen to the other person's response. Preparation is crucial; they must make it clear to the church officer what they want from him, but not expect him to make any decisions or provide them with any specific opportunities. Rather, they should ask him to coach them, moving in directions that will result in victory for both the church and themselves.

Lauren needs to realize that God made no mistake in creating her as he did. She does fit. It may be wise for her to clarify her position on the male headship issue with her pastor. If he knows that she has no intentions of trying to change the church's position, he can become her advocate, helping her find appropriate avenues of ministry.

Anne, too, should clarify her intentions. The elders need to know of her willingness to serve on the committee and work in partnership with the chairperson and other members to bring about innovation in the Christian education programs in the church.

Lauren and Anne's circumstances provide the opportunity to demonstrate and extend their leadership skills. Looking back at some of the characteristics of leaders, we see that both Lauren and Anne have lost sight of the *vision*, their goals, in the middle of frustration about *implementation*, how to accomplish their goals. The leader's challenge is to stay focused, as did Hannah and to develop new options for utilizing leadership skills.

Lauren might create a group within her church for professional and career women. If there are not enough women within her church an inter-denominational or community group would be in order. Such a group might prove to be a powerful new outreach.

Lauren might explore needs for information gathering and processing (her professional expertise) within the church, and volunteer to put together any systems that are needed in this area. This would enable her to use her skills, work with other volunteers, and become a visible, contributing member of the church.

Anne might volunteer to serve on the Christian education committee, not as its chairperson, but as a member. Since a new chairperson must be selected, and the job is obviously a very large one, this would be an ideal time for her to offer her support.

Anne might become a project-design leader, rather than be appointed to an ongoing leadership position. This option, widely used in business organizations in which special skills are needed, even if only temporarily, will allow Anne to demonstrate her leadership style, showing others that she is collaborative, not subversive.

NEXT STEPS FOR MEN IN
OFFICES OF AUTHORITY

These situations offer the male leadership in the church opportunities to reexamine their goals and motives. The first step for them, as it is for Lauren and Anne, is to prayerfully examine the situations before them. Their prayers should focus on how the Lord wants them to work with the variety of gifts in the body he has entrusted to their leadership.

Churches must be willing to make creative adjustments if they are going to recognize the gifts and release the energy of women like Lauren and Anne. Our observation is that often it is not the biblical principle that is the issue. While there are some who think women should serve only in the kitchen and the nursery, the great majority of evangelical men honestly desire to fully employ the gifts of women. The problem comes in deciding how. Men need to move beyond a *willingness* to employ women's gifts in ministry and become *advocates* for women, thus empowering them to serve in more capacities within the traditional male-headship structure.

After all, what is wrong with a woman's serving on a church committee, or even chairing the committee, when she is under the authority of the governing body of the church? If the only person in the church with a degree in Christian education is a woman, and the educational program is floundering, does it make sense not to employ her expertise? It does not seem to us that the principle of male headship has to be violated to allow a woman to serve as chairperson of a committee.

If there is a need for a class on marriage, and there is a Christian marriage counselor in the congregation, should the church fail to use her skills because she is a woman? The biblical principle of male headship in the church is not in jeopardy if the woman holds to the doctrinal position of the church and is willing to serve under men ordained to positions of authority.

Here are some other suggestions that might be considered.

Many churches have found that women who serve on the worship committee help design worship services that often add warmth and diversity. Because worship services incorporate our minds, wills, and emotions in the worship of our sovereign God, women, who are often more feeling-oriented than are men, make ideal designers. In too many churches, the same order of worship is followed every Sunday. Many pastors have neither the time nor the inclination to do anything more than change the hymn numbers, while many women long to give help in this area. How much more meaningful it would be for the congregation if women were used to plan a variety of worship experiences.

Many pastors bemoan the fact that too few people do all of the work. Often these pastors have not been trained to develop and employ the human resources in their churches, yet there may be women whose training and/or inclinations have equipped them to develop a system to track the interests and involvement of every member of the church. The nurturing strengths of women often give them energy and sensitivity for this task.

Women in education, whether public school, Christian school, or home school, are valuable in teaching situations. In addition they have expertise that should be used in planning educational programs. By serving on committees or as coordinators of programs, they can give needed depth and direction to the teaching, discipleship ministry of the church. Professional women have other skills that many churches need desperately. Skills in planning, motivating, and training are surely useful in the church.

The helper verses mentioned earlier that refer to God's concern for the victim, the fatherless, the needy, and the afflicted are relevant to our society. Churches cannot remain removed from these issues and be lights in the world. Women, with their capacity to care for and attach themselves to others, can develop and implement ministries to reach out to abuse victims, throw-away teens, the homeless, the lonely, etc. The key seems to be willingness on the part of women to function under the authority of the male leadership, and willingness on the part of the male leadership to allow room for these women to serve in appropriate yet innovative ways.

STRATEGY FOR THE WOMEN'S MINISTRY

A dynamic women's ministry that is seeking to mobilize women to minister to one another and to collectively address ministry opportunities in the church and community will see women like Lauren and Anne as wonderful resources. Too often women feel threatened by other women. There are many misconceptions: Women employed outside the home assume disapproval from those who have been able to choose to remain at home, while those who are not employed outside the home sense, from those who are employed, that the stay-at-home women are lazy and unproductive. This is unfortunate. The strategy for a sensitive women's ministry will be to seek ways to encourage communication and understanding between women in different circumstances and different seasons of life. Panel discussions that include women in a variety of situations talking openly about what they need from other women, how they are creatively serving the Lord, and about their frustrations and victories, give women opportunities to learn from and support one another. Leadership in a women's ministry offers women with administrative and organizational skills a viable place to use their skills to creatively help other women.

Many times women like Lauren and Anne feel they don't fit into the women's ministries in their church, and the other women assume they are not interested. However, when the Laurens and the Annes are asked to take leadership positions that match their gifts and experiences, we have seen women's ministries come alive under their leadership.

LEADERSHIP SKILLS FOR WOMEN

Even though all kinds of leadership skills might apply to the needs discussed in this chapter, three stand out as being particularly important: persuasion, motivation, and organization.

Persuasion is the ability to get others to support you and have them believe it was *their* idea. The skill of persuasion is one of the most powerful additions to a women's skills repertoire. To move others to your side, you need first ask the questions, "Why would this person want to support me? What's in it for them?" Then, like any good salesperson, you should use this information in order to sell the benefits of your proposal or idea. Benefits are advantages to the other person, *not to you.* These benefits help others see how doing what you want them to do helps you both accomplish the same goal.

The most persuasive people are those who are able to develop strong, graphic word pictures. Compare these two paragraphs that describe the very same thing.

Today's church leader must be able to think beyond today to the future. He or she must be creative in the development of new perspectives that add value to the group.

Think of the new church leader as the designer of the future. The new leader works with bold, colorful brush strokes—not with the narrow black and white line of the traditional pencil-and-paper leader.

Your practical self may prefer the first version, but your imaginative, intuitive self will always be drawn to the word-picture language of the second version. Whenever you are writing or planning what to say, go back and ask yourself how you can use word pictures to add imagery, excitement, and force to your words.

Motivation is the next critical leadership skill. People are motivated either to avoid something that they do not want or to seek something that they do want. Traditionally these have been known as the "carrot" or the "stick" approaches to motivation. At one time we believed that punishment (the stick) was the way to get people to do what we wanted. Now, however, behavioral scientists largely conclude that people are more likely to do what we want when we use a carrot (incentive).

Think of the times that you have been truly motivated to tackle very difficult tasks. These are likely to be times when you were so committed to the results that obstacles did not seem important, or times when you were feeling so good about yourself and the contributions you could make that your energy was continuously renewed. Skilled leaders paint such vivid pictures of the possible results that others are motivated to join the effort and then they support and encourage in ways that provide everyone with energy and purpose for the task.

A wonderful illustration of this is told by Ted Engstrom in *The Speaker's Sourcebook.** Years ago there was a group of brilliant young men at the University of Wisconsin who seemed to have amazing creative literary talent. They were would-be poets, novelists, and essayists who made the best possible use of the English language. These promising young men met regularly to read and critique each other's work. And critique it they did!

---

*Van Ekeren, Glen, ed., *The Speaker's Sourcebook*, (New York: Prentice-Hall), 1988.

They were merciless with one another. They dissected the most minute literary expression into a hundred pieces. They were heartless, tough, even mean in their criticism. The sessions became such arenas of literary criticism that the members of this exclusive club called themselves the Stranglers.

Not to be outdone, the women students who had literary talent were determined to start a club of their own, one comparable to the Stranglers. They called themselves the Wranglers. They, too, read their works to one another. But there was one great difference—the criticism was much softer, more positive, and more encouraging. Sometimes, there was almost no criticism at all. Every effort, even the most feeble one, was encouraged.

Twenty years later an alumnus of the university was doing an exhaustive study of his classmates' careers when he noticed a vast difference in the literary accomplishments of the Stranglers as opposed to the Wranglers. Of all the bright young men in the Stranglers, not one had made a significant literary contribution of any kind. From the Wranglers had come six or more successful writers such as Marjorie Kinnan Rawlings who wrote *The Yearling*.

What was the difference between these two groups? Talent? Both groups had about the same talent. Education? Not much difference here either. The difference was that the Stranglers strangled while the Wranglers were determined to uplift each other. The Stranglers promoted an atmosphere of contention and self-doubt. The Wranglers emphasized the strengths of each member of the group.

Leaders need to be Wranglers, motivating others through confidence-building, coaching, and encouragement.

In addition to persuasion and motivation, skills that are part of managing other people associated with projects, leaders themselves need to be able to competently take on and accomplish tasks. This skill of organization is important because every project requires planning and doing.

Organization is critical and requires that one carefully think through each aspect of a task and lay it out in logical sequence.

The first step in organizing is to make sure that all the resources are in place for doing what needs to be done. For example, if you do not have plenty of envelopes, labels, and fillers, getting an important mailer out will not be easy to accomplish.

The second aspect of organization is to carefully follow-up to make sure that each task needing to be done is done well. For example, checklists, invaluable in planning and organizing projects, are also invaluable in helping make sure that every small detail has been taken care of. Organization is the skill that simultaneously takes care of both the big picture and the small details.

THE BOTTOM LINE

After listing great heros and heroines of the faith whose lives made positive statements for the kingdom, the author of Hebrews gives us a compelling image of the Christian life:

> Therefore, since we are surrounded by such a great cloud of witnesses, let us throw off everything that hinders and the sin that so easily entangles, and let us run with perseverance the race marked out for us. Let us fix our eyes on Jesus, the author and perfecter of our faith, who for the joy set before him endured the cross, scorning its shame, and sat down at the right hand of the throne of God. Consider him who endured such opposition from sinful men, so that you will not grow weary and lose heart. (Heb. 12:1-3)

We cannot escape it. Focusing on Jesus rather than our circumstances will enable us to run the race with wisdom. Notice that it is not the responsibility of the runner to determine the course of the race. We are to run the race that our sovereign God sets before us with Jesus as our model. His course was not easy. . .in fact at one point he asked if it was possible that the course be changed, but he immediately added, "Yet not as I will, but as you will" (Matt. 26:39). By staying on course, he had to endure the Cross. But what looked like defeat actually brought about the greatest change in history—the restoration of a relationship between God and his people.

To be women who make a difference, whose lives make a positive statement for the kingdom, we must not allow ourselves to get sidetracked by trying to change the direction of our race. This will cause so much confusion that we will be running in circles. Our energy must be expended in fixing our eyes on Jesus as we run with perseverance. We can trust the direction and the difficulty of the course to our Father. This is an exciting race because we are assured of the ultimate prize. And who knows but what our apparent defeats may be used of God to bring about positive change?

Our race is not a solo race. We must develop and use our skills to enlist others to run alongside. Positive persuasion and motivation create an environment that makes others want to run with us. Well-developed organization keeps the race plan realistic and always before us, enabling us to run the race wisely.

What is the most creative approach when it comes to dealing with the barriers that seemingly restrict us from exercising our gifts in the church? Should we fight, flee, or wait prayerfully?

Hannah, who wisely chose to prayerfully wait on the Lord, had the joy of seeing her son faithfully minister before the Lord. Each year when she went with her husband up to Shiloh to offer the annual sacrifice,

> Eli would bless Elkanah and his wife, saying, "May the LORD give you children by this woman to take the place of the one she prayed for and gave to the LORD." Then they would go home. And the LORD was gracious to Hannah; she conceived and gave birth to three sons and two daughters. Meanwhile, the boy Samuel grew up in the presence of the LORD. (1 Sam. 2:20–21)

Fight, flight, or prayerful waiting . . . ? We rest our case!

> Who is wise and understanding among you? Let him show it by his good life, by deeds done in the humility that comes from wisdom. (James 3:13)

But the wisdom that comes from heaven is first of all pure; then peace-loving, considerate, submissive, full of mercy and good fruit, impartial and sincere. (James 3:17)

If any of you lacks wisdom, he should ask God, who gives generously to all without finding fault, and it will be given to him. (James 1:5)

CHAPTER SEVEN

Confidence

7

Glorify the LORD with me: let us exalt his name together (Psalm 34:3).

I can do everything through him who gives me strength (Phil. 4:13).

GOAL: To help women identify and interpret internal barriers, i.e., poor self-concept, guilt, failure to recognize their opportunities and abilities, false interpretation of perceived weaknesses.

       To help women understand that the confidence that comes through Christ is the biblical remedy for overcoming these barriers.

       To challenge the church to develop a loving, safe environment where women are given opportunities to grow in Christ-confidence and develop ministry skills.

LIFE EXAMPLES

"What should we do?" the chairperson of the nominating committee asked Jane. "We are grateful that you have agreed to be president of the women's ministry, but we can't find anyone to assume the other offices. Should we eliminate some of our activities? We meet only once a month, and yet our attendance is dwindling. The women in our church seem to lack commitment in serving the Lord." Jane knows that the nominating committee is discouraged. She knows, too, that she feels called of the Lord to serve as president. Jane feels that God has given her a genuine love for the women in her church and an increasing desire to see them mobilized for ministry. Let's look in on some of the women in Jane's church and try to discover the real problem.

Betsy closes her Bible and opens her church bulletin to pray for the various activities at church that day. She notices that the nominating committee for the women's ministry is meeting. Betsy knows they are having difficulty finding women to assume offices. "Father," she prays, "You know how I would like to be involved in this ministry. You know, too, how painful it is for me to even walk into a roomful of women. I feel as if they can look right inside of me and see what is really there." Betsy is convinced that if the other women knew that before she became a Christian she had had an abortion, they would never accept her. She longs to develop her gifts and serve the Savior she loves, but she feels uncomfortable whenever she is with the women in her church.

A few blocks away, Mrs. Johnson reads the announcement in the church newsletter asking women to pray about becoming involved in the women's ministry. She looks at the empty chair beside her and wishes she could talk and pray about this with Dan. Before he died six months ago, Mr. Johnson was an invalid who needed his wife's care. Through this experience Mrs. Johnson has learned much about the faithfulness of God and the power of prayer and has entered into a new dimension of dependence on the Lord. But, she wonders if she can regain the confidence and the energy she would need to assume a position of responsibility.

Sarah puts the morning paper down, takes the last sip of coffee, and wonders what she can do to fill the day. Since her last child left for college, Sarah finds it increasingly difficult to get motivated. She has not worked outside the home in the twenty-five years since her first child was born. Before this she was an assistant buyer for a large retail chain. She has a degree in marketing and was at one time considered to have a great deal of talent in fashion merchandising. She aimlessly picks up the church newsletter and notices the announcement asking if anyone has suggestions for the women's ministry. "I wish I were creative enough to think of something—they sure need it," she thinks as she puts the newsletter aside. She decides to see if she can find someone who will go shopping with her.

Three cars are parked in Laura's driveway. Three young mothers are kissing their children good-bye as Laura cheerfully kisses them hello. Laura keeps these children so that she can remain at home with her baby and so that these single moms in her church can know that their children are in a safe, Christian environment. None of these young women has even had time to read the church newsletter, though they have discussed their feelings about not being involved in the women's ministry. They feel the older women are disappointed in them, but the meetings are so irrelevant to their day-to-day lives that it is difficult to make the effort to attend.

After watching the morning news on television, Mrs. Baker closes the door of her room so that she can have her daily devotion time with the Lord. She loves the Savior dearly, and she wishes she could still serve him. She feels so useless since moving to the nursing home. Her mind is still alert, but her body is weak.

In contrast, Judy listens to the same newscast as she quickly dresses and gulps down an instant breakfast drink. Driving to her job as a secretary in a large corporation, she thinks about how lonely and detached she feels from other women at church since going back to work. She wishes she could still be involved in the women's ministry. A part of her wishes she didn't need to work, but with two children in college, the family needs extra income. Then she begins praying that the Lord will give her wisdom to comfort Lisa, her coworker who is going through a divorce.

Shannon, a single woman, is already at her desk. Shannon is successful in her career and loves the church she recently joined. Still she wishes there was some way to connect with other Christian women. The monthly women's circles are made up of married women, and she just doesn't believe she would fit.

Unfortunately, Jane doesn't know the thoughts and feelings of any of these other women. Still the nominating committee is looking to her for answers! Jane thinks about the lessons she has been learning from her study of Queen Esther. "Perhaps the problem is not a lack of commitment but the lack of confidence," she muses. "Maybe we haven't asked the right women in the right way—the women God has chosen 'for such a time as this.'"

LESSONS FROM SCRIPTURE

Esther was far more than just a pretty face. Her classic statement, "If I perish, I perish" (Est. 4:16), reveals that she was a woman of discipline, determination, and devotion to the God of Israel. How did she develop such confidence?

There are many beautiful lessons in the story of Esther. But, for our purposes let us jump right in at the middle when wicked Haman manipulated Esther's husband into issuing an edict to destroy all of the Jews living in his kingdom. Neither King Xerxes nor Haman was aware of Esther's Jewish identity, because she had been instructed by her cousin Mordecai to keep this facet of her life a secret.

The edict was issued; there was bewilderment and alarm throughout the kingdom. Mordecai put on sackcloth and walked through the city wailing loudly. When Esther, who was unaware of the edict, heard that Mordecai was dressed in sackcloth, she instructed her servant to find out what was troubling him.

Mordecai sent a copy of the king's edict to Esther and urged her to go to the king and beg for mercy for her people. Esther understandably hesitated—not only would this action reveal her Jewish identity, but going unsummoned to the king would mean death unless the king held out his gold scepter. Esther sent word back to Mordecai that it had been thirty days since the king had summoned her.

Mordecai, however, persisted, and we believe the key to Esther's confidence is found in his challenge to her.

> Do not think that because you are in the king's house you alone of all the Jews will escape. For if you remain silent at this time, relief and deliverance for the Jews will arise from another place, but you and your father's family will perish.

> And who knows but that you have come to royal position for
> such a time as this? (Est. 4:13–14)

Esther rose to the occasion and replied, "I will go to the king, even though it is against the law. And if I perish, I perish" (v. 16).

We often think that the power of Mordecai's challenge is in the words, "And who knows but that you have come to royal position for such a time as this?" A significant place in history is often a forceful incentive, but perhaps the real confidence builder for Esther is his opening remark: "If you remain silent at this time, relief and deliverance for the Jews *will arise* from another place. . . ."

Mordecai was reminding his cousin of God's faithfulness to his covenant promise. Mordecai's confidence that deliverance would arise must have reminded Esther of all she had learned from him about the character of Jehovah. The Sovereign God who had entered into a covenant relationship with Abraham would not allow his people to be annihilated. He had made promises and he would be faithful to keep those promises. Mordecai believed that deliverance would come with or without Esther. Esther could seize this opportunity to be used of God, or she could miss her moment. Esther hesitated when she thought of the danger, but Mordecai's reminder quickly refocused her on kingdom thinking.

Esther made a decision to obey God. She confidently made that decision because of her knowledge of God. Her availability was based on God's reliability. Once she had made her decision, Esther moved quickly to the next step. Neither the immensity nor the immediacy of the problem kept her from calling on her people to fast and focus on God for three days. Esther knew the power of prayer, and she would not operate alone—she sought the prayer support of the people of God.

Esther must have displayed great confidence as she dressed in her royal robes to go before the king. However, we do not believe this confidence came from Esther herself: It came from God.

When our confidence is based on God, we are able to think, act, and speak biblically. Our confidence is based upon who he is and what he has done—he is the King and he has given us a position in his kingdom. We view our abilities and circumstances, whatever they may be, as opportunities designed by the Sovereign King for the advancement of his kingdom.

Consider the genius of Mordecai in motivating his young cousin to make herself available for kingdom work.

First notice what he did **not** do.

He did not devastate her by rebuking her, "If you were really committed you would not hesitate to assume this responsibility."

Neither did he use guilt, "I've done so much for you—you really owe me."

Nor did he build up a false confidence by focusing on her own abilities, accomplishments, or circumstance, "Esther you are so successful and loved—you can do it!"

Mordecai wisely realized that the overwhelming importance and danger of this situation was beyond Esther's internal resources. He instilled confidence in Esther by focusing her on the person and promises of God and by surrounding her with the prayers of God's people. This formula positioned Esther to confidently serve God and his people, and this helper/leader became the advocate for the victims and the afflicted.

The New Testament elaborates on this formula by showing that our weakness is actually our point of strength, because it is our weakness that has the potential to press us into dependence upon God.

> But he said to me, "My grace is sufficient for you, for my power is made perfect in weakness." Therefore I will boast all the more gladly about my weaknesses, so that Christ's power may rest on me. That is why, for Christ's sake, I delight in weaknesses, in insults, in hardships, in persecutions, in difficulties. For when I am weak, then I am strong. (2 Cor. 12:9–10)

The writer of Hebrews continues to develop this theme and points out the necessity of a vertical relationship with the

105

Father as the source of confidence to serve. He adds to it the importance of horizontal relationships with believers. After giving a clear description of our position in Christ there is a powerful **therefore**. Jesus is our high priest. . . . He has made the perfect, once-for-all-time sacrifice. . . . We have confidence to enter the Most Holy Place and assurance of our position in the kingdom because of who he is and what he has done in our place. . . **therefore**—because of this confidence in the vertical relationship we have with the Father—we are to stimulate and motivate one another on toward love and good deeds (Heb. 10:19–25).

We need a context, a greenhouse, in which this confidence can grow and develop. God lovingly placed us in the church and instructed us to give careful thought to how we can spur one another on toward love and good deeds. To be sure that we understand the importance of our responsibility to one another in developing this confidence to serve, the writer of Hebrews follows through by saying, "Let us not give up meeting together, as some are in the habit of doing, but let us encourage one another" (v. 25).

Women like those described at the beginning of this chapter need to be stimulated to discover and encouraged to develop their gifts. Some women need others to help them interpret their circumstances and translate their particular combination of circumstances and abilities into ministry. Too often we assume that lack of involvement is equal to lack of commitment. We, however, are convinced that often the problem is not lack of commitment but a lack of confidence. So how can we create a safe environment where women will have the confidence to develop ministry skills?

Let us return to Mordecai and Esther and take a closer look at their relationship.

When Esther was orphaned, Scripture tells us that Mordecai took her into his home and treated her as his own daughter. He did not see her as a burden. This father-daughter relationship must have been very tender and affirming for Esther.

We know little about how or why Esther was chosen to be a

106

part of the beauty contest to find a queen for King Xerxes other than the fact that she was very beautiful. We do know that Mordecai did not desert her during this difficult time. We also know that she continued to trust Mordecai's judgment.

> Esther had not revealed her nationality and family background, because Mordecai had forbidden her to do so. Every day he walked back and forth near the courtyard of the harem to find out how Esther was and what was happening to her. (Est. 2:10–11)

It seems to us that these two sentences reveal a powerful relationship. Mordecai's deep concern for Esther cannot be missed; neither can we overlook her trust in him. Mordecai must have viewed this nerve-racking situation through a faith that assured him that somehow it would all work together for good.

By lovingly accepting this little orphan as a daughter, and not abandoning her when she left his home, Mordecai positioned himself to motivate Esther at a time when she was needed for kingdom work. He made an investment in her life and he must have believed that God had sovereignly placed Esther under his care, because he poured enormous energy into helping her become what God wanted her to be. His eventual challenge to her was not given in a vacuum but in the context of a relationship of love, acceptance, trust, and commitment.

When Esther eventually went before the king to plead for her people, the king held out his gold scepter. Her skillful management throughout this situation is stunning. She did not become hysterical. When asked what she wanted, Esther calmly invited the king to a banquet. Following that party she invited the king to a second banquet after which she promised to state her petition. The king was so enamored with his queen that he begged her to present her request to him: "Queen Esther, what is your petition? It will be given you. What is your request? Even up to half the kingdom, it will be granted" (Est. 7:2).

Esther calmly presented her case and the king listened. Since his first edict could not be reversed, he granted Esther and Mordecai permission to author another decree giving the

Jews the right to assemble and protect themselves. Wicked Haman, who had devised the plot, hanged, and Mordecai was given a place of prominence in the kingdom.

As the story progresses, the relationship between Mordecai and Esther seems to change. We believe this change again reveals Mordecai's genius in helping Esther develop her potential. The remaining events of the story show Esther and Mordecai working side by side to save the Jews from annihilation. It seems that they moved from a father-daughter relationship to a partnership. Mordecai wisely recognized Esther's maturity. She was no longer a little girl. He did not need to give her instructions; they could collaborate.

Mordecai is an example that churches should emulate in creating an environment where others will be stimulated to love and good deeds. The following is a good guide.

- Make an investment in another person's life by establishing a relationship of love and acceptance.
- Present the opportunity for kingdom service.
- Focus on the person and promises of God.
- Surround the person with the prayers of God's people.

This formula, used by Mordecai, positioned Esther to confidently serve God and his people as a helper-leader.

When the male and female leadership in a church put their energy into nurturing before they assign tasks, there will be a deeper intimacy in the church family. This intimacy will permeate every fiber of the church life and will help people overcome internal barriers that inhibit the development and use of their spiritual gifts.

NEXT STEPS FOR WOMEN

Women often play a game called "Not. . .Enough." You know what it is—"I'm not smart enough, quick enough, strong enough, old enough, young enough, patient enough, organized enough, etc." Even though we all recognize, at least at some level, the uselessness of this game, we all seem to play it. Thus, our response to a need is too often based on our perceived weaknesses rather than on our actual strengths. Coach John Wooden of UCLA said it well, "Do not let what you cannot do interfere with what you can do."

The first step for all the women in our Life Example is to spend time honestly appraising what they *can* do. Each of these women has some specific abilities, based on her gifts, her experiences, her temperaments, and her stage in life. It is important for us to spend some quiet time meditating on our strengths—it is not arrogant to do so. Our strengths are gifts from the Lord. We need to focus on how they can be used to serve others.

Next, each of these women needs to recognize that when the Lord has put a burden on her heart, whether it is for stepping forward and saying, "Maybe I can do that," or for sharing a deep personal pain, he will support her fully. Prayer is the most powerful tool here, but sharing with a trusted Christian friend can magnify the answers to prayer.

It is no accident that the women portrayed in the opening scenes of this chapter are where they are at this particular point in time. Like Esther, they must realize that they have been chosen for "such a time as this," whatever that may be. When they turn the circumstances of their lives over to the Lord, they can say with confidence, "I will go. . . ."

If Betsy, Mrs. Johnson, Sarah, and the others could look around them for opportunities, they might see the places where their needs overlap. We are placed in families and in larger communities because God created us as beings dependent on one another. This dependency is not negative. It is a powerful force that links generations and their changing needs and produces mutual support. My (Peggy's) father, a retired widower, after seeing his frantically busy daughter, commented wisely that the Lord gives us what seems to be either too much to do or too little to do in different stages of life, perhaps to see *how* we will do it.

NEXT STEPS FOR MEN IN
OFFICES OF AUTHORITY

Men in leadership positions need to develop open minds about everyone in their congregations—men *and* women. Open-minded views that are free of stereotypes are truly difficult to achieve. In fact they are *humanly* impossible.

Surveys that assess gifts, experiences, and desires to serve are useful, but not nearly as useful as regular discussions about personal needs and opportunities. However, regular discussions cannot take place without appropriate training in interpersonal skills for those in authority. This training, then, along with "opportunity" meetings will assure that indecision or poor self-esteem—common blocks to filling out surveys honestly and completely—do not get in the way. By instituting ongoing, one-on-one discussions in order to match gifts, experiences, and desires to serve with service opportunities, we will help more people overcome barriers that inhibit ministry to the body of Christ.

Encourage everyone to have a ministry—one thing they can do, regardless of how many things the cannot do—and to pursue it faithfully. Officers have a wider perspective of congregational needs and should be able to match givers and receivers.

It is also important for church officers to express appreciation, both privately and publicly, for all women. Rejoice in the diversity within your congregation. Most likely any specific church is made up of women who are single, women who are single moms, women who homeschool their children, women who make a living outside the home, women who remain home for their children, and women who are widows. All of these women are important and each can contribute in her own way. Take time to tell each one that she brings special value to your church. Pray publicly for each group and encourage both the women and the body at large to realize the value of each of the parts.

This book is about women, but all members need recognition and support—regardless of who they are or what they may have done. The male leadership of a church must put energy into encouraging and developing all of the laity.

STRATEGY FOR THE WOMEN'S MINISTRY

The five ideas for forming or strengthening the women's ministry described in chapter 4 are also applicable here. In addition, an anonymously completed survey for women may be helpful. Anonymity may free some women to reveal private needs—including whether they have suffered any kind of abuse, whether they have suffered addiction to a controlled substance, whether they are experiencing guilt, and whether they have other needs they would like to have met by the women's ministry. Then develop programs to meet these needs.

Determine the women who are not involved and target them *for* ministry. Do not ask them to do something for you; ask what you can do for them. If young women are not involved, invite several to join two or three officers of the women's ministry for lunch. Ask them how you can minister to them; how you can meet their needs; what you can contribute to them. Cultivate a relationship of genuine caring and concern before you ask them to become involved or assume responsibilities. Listen to what they say and then design appropriate programs to meet their needs. A women's ministry is on track when it begins to follow Mordecai's formula for motivating women to kingdom service. Many women are not self-starters, but they would be willing to serve if they were approached in an encouraging way. Women in leadership have the precious privilege of incorporating women who are in various seasons and circumstances of life into the church's women's ministry.

We are increasingly convinced that accomplishing this blending and use of women requires weekly Bible studies. It is difficult to establish and nurture relationships when you meet only once a month. Many women are longing for close friendships with other women and need to meet weekly.

Weekly gatherings also allow for more involvement in

ministry. Women who minister together bond together. One model that is proving to be effective for many groups is to use one meeting each month as a ministry day. Offer several ministry outlets. Evangelism visitation, encouragement visitation (church members who are sick, elderly, etc.), community involvement (homeless shelter, nursing home, crisis pregnancy center, etc.), and cross-cultural ministry (international-student coffee at a local college, English classes for wives of foreign businessmen) are only a few of the possible ministries. Women can sign up for a different ministry each quarter or remain in the same one. It is important to provide enough variety so that every woman will feel comfortable with at least one ministry. Many women want to be involved in ministry, but they are not initiators. They would never venture out alone, but they will gladly go with a group.

Home schoolers and their children can be invited to join you on the ministry day. This sends the message that you care about what they are doing. Women who are no longer physically able to get out can be enlisted as prayer supporters for young mothers. Women employed outside the home can be encouraged to find coworkers who will join them for a brown-bag lunch and Bible study with the women's ministry providing a Bible teacher. The employed women are then a vital part of the women's ministry.

LEADERSHIP SKILLS FOR WOMEN

Women who are struggling with very real barriers, both in the world around them and within themselves, that prevent them from fully serving should focus on two critical leadership skills: positive self-concept and purposeful communications.

We believe that God intended for us to feel good about the unique features that he created within each of us. He intended for us to have healthy egos that enable us to recognize that we have skills, abilities, and a sense of purpose. It is not negative to identify and value the positive qualities you have been given by your Maker. Yet many Christian women suffer from poor self-concepts and seem to believe that feeling good about how God has created them is somehow arrogant.

To develop, or maintain a healthy self-concept, try some of these activities:

1. Face a mirror and talk to yourself. Vocalize as many positive qualities (skills, traits, interests, etc.) as you can think of. You may feel very awkward, but if you keep at it you should be able to complete quite a list.

Speak strongly and confidently—convince even yourself what a wonderful creature God created when he created you. Include both those qualities you know you have and the ones that others have attributed to you—even if you are not so sure that you agree with them. (Avoid negative judgments—especially subtle ones. "I have some of that ability, but not nearly as much as Joan, nor as much as I'd like to have" is negative thinking.)

2. Meet with a small group of other women for a "strength bombardment." Sit in a circle and select one person to be "it." Then for two minutes, everyone in the group bombards the woman who is it with things they admire or respect about her. In turn, each woman will be it and will hear only positive comments for two full minutes.

3. Make a written list of your strengths. Select one item from this list each day to pray about. Ask God to help you develop this strength, and to use it confidently for his glory.

Purposeful communication allows us to accomplish our goals simply and straightforwardly; it helps separate emotional diversions from our real goals; and it builds others up, makes honest and direct requests, puts expectations in motivating terms, and avoids whining, complaining, and tearing others down. Two important keys to purposeful communications are:

1. Plan your communications. Talk to yourself the way you might talk to others, and then really listen. After that, rephrase whatever you have said in two or three other ways to strengthen its impact. Finally, select the approach you believe will be the strongest for accomplishing your goals.

2. Talk in positive, hopeful terms. This might sound as if

you are playing word games, but it can be powerful to take what might be your natural tendency to talk about the difficulties or problems (e.g., "people just won't do what they say they will"), and describe them in terms of opportunities (e.g., "this is a real opportunity for me to practice my coaching and follow-through skills").

These keys to purposeful communications are not necessarily easily accomplished. If you practice them, however, you will find that your leadership skills increase dramatically because others want to follow!

THE BOTTOM LINE

Instead of playing the "Not. . .Enough" game we talked about earlier, let's play "What If. . ."

What if Jane (the women's ministry president in the example) used the ideas set out in this chapter to form a women's ministry that provided a safe place for women in which to cultivate friendships, build positive self-concepts, and become involved in significant ministry.

What if. . .

- After a program featuring a panel of women who had suffered abuse or addiction, Betsy were to feel free to share her burden with others and this purposeful communication released her from guilt and freed her to join other women in working at a crisis pregnancy center?
- Mrs. Johnson and several other widows were invited to have coffee with Jane and this resulted in a support group for widows and in a ministry by widows to home teachers?
- Sarah were challenged to use her fashion-marketing skills to plan the special features for the women's quarterly outreach brunches and she used her knowledge of the industry to bring in a fashion consultant, a crafts demonstration, and other programs that would become "entry points" for unchurched friends?

114

- One of the weekly Bible leaders were to teach a lesson at a local restaurant at 7:00 A.M. for Judy and her co-workers? What if the young mothers who left their children at Laura's joined the early-morning Bible Study and Sarah (remember, she had *lots* of free time) were there to help Laura get all of the children to church so that she, too, could participate in this dynamic women's ministry?
- Mrs. Baker were challenged to pray for a different church family each day to write a note of encouragement to that family?

What if you were a part of this exciting ministry?

But what if right now the life of the women's ministry in your church is in jeopardy?

Relief and deliverance for that ministry will arise. What if *you* have come to the kingdom for such a time as this!

CHAPTER EIGHT

Unity

8

*Glorify the LORD with me: let us exalt his name
together* (Psalm 34:3).

May the God who gives endurance and encouragement
give you a spirit of unity among yourselves as you
follow Christ Jesus, so that with one heart and mouth
you may glorify the God and Father of our Lord Jesus
Christ. Accept one another, then, just as Christ
accepted you, in order to bring praise to God (Rom.
15:5–7).

GOAL: To provide information and insights that will help
women create an environment of support and encouragement.
To consider the influence of women in helping maintain
the unity given by Christ in the church.

LIFE EXAMPLES

Jack, the pastor, could not understand what was going on.
He had never known the officers of the church to have so much
dissension among themselves. They all seemed to be discouraged and could only see the negative side of the issues before

them. Even the apparently simple decision to begin a Mother's Morning Out program had brought raised voices and heated conversation. Finally Jack suggested that they take a break. He was thankful for the telephone call he had received that afternoon from Mrs. Jackson, a widow in the congregation, who had volunteered to come and make a pot of coffee for the men.

Everyone walked in silence to the kitchen. Again, Jack breathed a prayer of thanksgiving for Mrs. Jackson. Beside the pot of coffee was a beautiful tray of homemade cookies, an array of cups, some sugar and creamer, and cheery napkins. "Enjoy!" read her note, "I am so thankful for godly men who are willing to serve our church. I will be in prayer for you as you meet. Leave your mess. It will be my privilege to clean it up."

The impact on the men was immediately obvious. They relaxed and began conversing among themselves about other things going on in their businesses and families. As they walked back into the meeting room, they were finally talking honestly and openly about the problems they had faced over the last few days that had colored their earlier participation in the meeting. Several of these outside events, it soon became apparent, had to do with relationships among the women in the church.

"Joan came home from the women's-ministry officers meeting in tears. She is so frustrated because of the friction among the women. She thought they were all backing her when they asked her to be an officer. Now she feels that her ideas and concerns are not even heard. Frankly, I'll be glad when her term of office is over," volunteered one man.

"I suppose it's because I'm a little older than some of you, but I've had calls from at least five of our women upset because we are considering a Mother's Morning Out program and have nothing planned for women who aren't young mothers," said another of the officers.

"My wife was hurt that not one of the women in the church called or came by during the time she was caring for her mother. She says no matter how long we are in the church, she will always feel like an outsider."

"I know about that," chimed in Jim. "My wife is a career

woman, and she believes that women can't really be accepted in this church until they're accepted by the group in the morning Bible study. Since she works every day, that leaves her out."

Ken, a young man who had recently been elected to serve as an elder, spoke up. "As I listen to what you are all saying, I realize that my wife has influenced my attitude. She feels that the older women in the church are disappointed with her. . .that she doesn't live up to their expectations of what an elder's wife should be. Several of the older women have made negative comments about her homeschooling our children and even about the fact that she is expecting our fifth child. She desperately needs the support of older women, yet she feels that our personal choices and her performance as the wife of an officer are unacceptable to these women. She needs approval, and she feels rejection. I am afraid this is affecting *her* attitude about my being an elder, and I *know* it is affecting my attitude.

As the men continued their discussion, it became apparent that—at least from their perspectives—the women in the church certainly did not support each other. Those women who were leaders in the women's programs, as well as those who exercised leadership in other areas of their lives, were not transferring their leadership skills to the church setting. This absence of good leadership affected the personal lives of these women, it affected the ministry of the women's group, and even negatively influenced the attitudes and behaviors of the men charged with managing the church and its programs.

The contrast between the atmosphere created by Mrs. Jackson with such a simple thing as a tray of refreshments and a note of gratitude, and the atmosphere these men had experienced because of negative words was astounding! Where was the breakdown that had created this negative atmosphere? Was it between the men and women? We believe that the real problem was not male-female; the real problem was female-female. There was a breakdown in the relationships among women in the church, and it was having a devastating effect.

I (Susan) have a quote written in calligraphy and framed in my kitchen. There is great truth in it:

*"If Mama ain't happy,
ain't nobody happy."*

Doesn't this speak eloquently of the power of a woman's influence? One of the things that keeps mama from being happy is the failure of her relationships with other women. Dr. James Dobson, a champion of the worth of women, notes that more women today are experiencing loneliness, depression, and problems in their marriages than was true in previous generations. He comments:

> A century ago, women cooked together, canned together, washed at the creek together, prayed together, went through menopause together, and grew old together. And when a baby was born, aunts and grandmothers and neighbors were there to show the new mother how to diaper and feed and discipline. Great emotional support was provided in this feminine contact. A woman was never really alone.

> Alas, the situation is very different today. The extended family has disappeared, depriving the wife of that source of security and fellowship. Her mother lives in New Jersey and her sister is in Texas. Furthermore, American families move every three or four years, preventing any long-term friendships from developing among neighbors. And there's another factor that is seldom admitted: American women tend to be economically competitive and suspicious of one another. Many would not even consider inviting a group of friends to the house until it was repainted, refurnished, or redecorated. As someone said, "We're working so hard to have beautiful homes and there's nobody in them!" The result is isolation—or should I say insulation—and its first cousin: loneliness.[1]

Dr. Dobson encourages women to "achieve a network of women friends with whom you can talk, laugh, gripe, dream, and recreate."[2]

---

[1]James C. Dobson, *Straight Talk to Men and Their Wives* (Waco: Word, 1984), 109.
[2]Ibid., 110.

LESSONS FROM SCRIPTURE

There are two sisters in Scripture who had an interesting relationship. These women appear to have been opposites in temperament and interest, and these differences caused friction. A closer look, however, reveals the development of a relationship that worked for them both. Our initial introduction to these women reveals a relationship that had broken down, but in a later episode we see a relationship that apparently emancipated them both to glorify God without their losing individual uniqueness. We can learn many lessons from Mary and Martha.

Most women are basically "Marys" or "Marthas"—relationship-oriented or task-oriented. Marys have a special ability to be sensitive to the needs and feelings of others, whereas Marthas are the ones who recognize what tasks need to be done and do them. Marys listen. . .Marthas talk. Marys meditate. . .Marthas delegate. Marys empathize. . .Marthas exercise. We need both in the church. The blend of these two temperaments gives balance to our ministry. But, rather than blending the uniqueness of each temperament to maintain unity, our tendency is to blast the differences. Result? Division.

Our unity in Christ is a gift from him, but we have a responsibility to *maintain* that unity. As Paul exhorts the Ephesians, "Make every effort to keep the unity of the Spirit through the bond of peace" (Eph. 4:3). It requires wisdom and an act of the will to maintain a spirit of unity and love—to be at peace with someone who sees and approaches life from a different perspective. Above all, it requires coming face to face with the realization of the person and the power of Jesus. We think that is what took place with Mary and Martha. Let's look in on what happened in their home and see what lessons we can learn.

> As Jesus and his disciples were on their way, he came to a village where a woman named Martha opened her home to him. She had a sister called Mary, who sat at the Lord's feet listening to what he said. But Martha was distracted by all

the preparations that had to be made. She came to him and asked, "Lord, don't you care that my sister has left me to do the work by myself? Tell her to help me!"

"Martha, Martha," the Lord answered, "you are worried and upset about many things, but only one thing is needed. Mary has chosen what is better, and it will not be taken away from her." (Luke 10:38–42)

Choices

We believe that Mary and Martha were both women of excellence who honestly longed to serve the Savior. They were thrilled when he chose to visit their home. Each woman expressed her excitement in her own way. Martha, the doer, saw it as an occasion for celebration, a time to have a party. Mary viewed the event from a totally different perspective: At last she could hear for herself the glorious words that fell from Jesus' lips.

Martha, without a moment's hesitation, began to plan her party. Not much had escaped this self-starter. (She had already taken the initiative to open her home to Jesus.) What a privilege for her to demonstrate her deep love and admiration for the Teacher by serving him. "Surely," she thought, "Mary will agree."

Mary, however, while she was probably thrilled that her sister had the confidence and boldness to open their home to Jesus, did not feel the same as Martha. Mary wanted to sit at Jesus' feet and watch his every movement, contemplate every nuance in his voice, and observe the perception in his eyes. Her absolute delight in his presence obliterated any consciousness of the responsibilities of hosting such a guest. We suspect that Mary was so enthralled that she was not even aware that Martha was busily making preparations for a meal.

There were choices to be made and each woman made her choice based on her perspective of the situation.

Jesus said, "Mary has chosen what is better. . . ." (Luke 10:42). Does that mean that Martha should not have prepared a meal? We don't think so. It was not wrong for Martha to exercise her gift of hospitality. In fact, it was necessary! No doubt Jesus and his disciples were hungry. The problem was that Martha proceeded without spending time with Jesus. The result was an unloving attitude. Activity without a loving attitude is not ministry.

As women of faith, we must understand that we make choices and set priorities daily. As believers, we do not act out of our old natures. We have been liberated by the power of Jesus. We can now choose our course of action. In speaking of choices, Paul says in Ephesians 1:3-4:

> Praise be to the God and Father of our Lord Jesus Christ, who has blessed us in the heavenly realms with every spiritual blessing in Christ. For he chose us in him before the creation of the world to be holy and blameless in his sight.

Because we have been chosen we have been freed from enslavement to sin and we can now make choices that bring praise to the God and Father of our Lord Jesus. Not only can we choose activities that are blameless in his sight, we can also choose to have attitudes that reflect the holiness of the Father. Christ gives us the ability to make these choices. Our first priority is to spend time with Christ so that his love will infuse our actions. Then we can serve with a loving spirit in the areas best suited to our gifts. This will produce a proper balance between piety and practice and will help us avoid disastrous distractions.

We can also choose to act in a spirit of love and unity by accepting and appreciating other people's choices. Negative statements about how others use their gifts strikes a destructive blow to unity, while positive statements create a climate in which unity flourishes.

Distractions

In the passage above we read that Martha became distracted by all that needed to be done and lost her focus. Doers often struggle with the proper order of piety and practice. They become so involved in the task that they begin focusing on *it* rather than on Jesus. To give value to what they are doing, they call attention to it. This is really no more than a subtle form of self-promotion or, to put it more bluntly, pride. The doer, as in Martha's case, creates an atmosphere of competition. "Lord, don't you care that my sister has left me to do the work by myself?" (Luke 10:40). How often we hear other forms of this same sentiment:

"I was in the nursery again this morning—no one else would keep it."

"The women who work outside the home just aren't interested in our women's ministry. They never participate in our activities or projects."

"The younger women never visit our members in the nursing home—all they want to do is have aerobics classes."

"The older women never help with fellowship suppers or the nursery. They say that they have served their time and now the younger women should assume these responsibilities."

These kinds of comments do not encourage others to line up to join in ministry!

Pride is a powerful distraction. The desire to be like God distracted Eve and destroyed the perfect atmosphere in her home. However, when our relationship with Jesus is a priority, then our service will not distract, but will attract. *We* will be attracted to him, and we will also attract *others* to him. By failing to quietly sit at the feet of Jesus, Martha's service became burdensome, and she became resentful and distracted, which resulted in the disruption of the spirit of love and unity in her home.

Expectations

Martha was intent on her project, and she expected Mary to be involved. However, once she was distracted from the thrill of serving Jesus by all that needed to be done, her attention quickly moved to the reality that Mary was not helping. Martha had unrealistic expectations of Mary and her disappointment degenerated into disapproval.

Disapproval is as devastating to the "disapprover" as it is to the one who fails to receive approval. The one who disapproves of others usually becomes discouraged with them and then discouraged with the Lord: "Lord, don't you care. . . ?" The one who is disapproved of also becomes discouraged. Fear and feelings of rejection breed in an atmosphere of disapproval.

Acceptance

Martha did not accept the ministry choice that Mary made. Martha's negative judgment caused her to become dissatisfied and irritated with Mary and critical of her Lord. She thought she had to instruct Jesus in how to handle the situation. When we do not accept the ministry choices of others, in effect we say, "She should be like me. She should serve in the same way I serve." This really expresses a lack of trust in the Lord in regard to his choice of the gifts he gives others, and a lack of trust in the Lord in regard to how he accomplishes his will through the gifts of others.

Acceptance frees people to develop their gifts. Lack of acceptance produces division. We maintain love and unity by choosing to be consumed with our attraction to our Lord and by trusting him to work in others to accomplish his purposes.

Did Martha learn these lessons? Did her relationship with her Lord and with her sister improve? We believe that she heard the gentle rebuke of Jesus and made a choice to submit to his Word. We know this from a later event when Jesus was making his way to Jerusalem for his final hour. Again he arrived at Bethany where a dinner was given in his honor. Let's look in on this very special occasion.

Six days before the Passover, Jesus arrived at Bethany, where Lazarus lived, whom Jesus had raised from the dead. Here a dinner was given in Jesus' honor. Martha served, while Lazarus was among those reclining at the table with him. Then Mary took about a pint of pure nard, an expensive perfume; she poured it on Jesus' feet and wiped his feet with her hair. And the house was filled with the fragrance of the perfume.

But one of his disciples, Judas Iscariot, who was later to betray him, objected. . . .

127

"Leave her alone," Jesus replied. "It was intended that
she should save this perfume for the day of my burial." (John
12:1–7)

Isn't it interesting that once again we find Martha serving
with no mention of Mary helping her. Even Lazarus is reclining
at the table. Martha seems to have been surrounded by non-
doers!

Though neither Lazarus nor Mary was engaged in any
practical activity, and Martha alone was involved in the tasks to
be done, she neither complained nor criticized. Jesus did not
rebuke Martha's choice of ministry. We find that Martha is still
the task-oriented member of the family, but apparently no
longer distracted. Perhaps her acceptance and approval of the
choices made by others freed her to serve Christ in love. Instead
of focusing on what Mary was, or was not, doing, she could
joyfully engage in her ministry of hospitality.

We wonder if Martha's acceptance and approval also freed
Mary to quietly perform a beautiful ministry—to lavish every
drop of that costly ointment on Jesus. The sensitive natures of
Marys enable them to interpret the reactions of others with
amazing accuracy. Surely Mary was not oblivious to Martha's
earlier disapproval and we believe Mary would have made every
effort to please her sister. We also have to believe that Martha
communicated an attitude of approval for Mary to have felt the
freedom to indulge in such a creative, yet costly, act of worship.

What freed Martha to accept and approve of the choices
made by others? What enabled her to create an atmosphere of
support and encouragement, allowing her sister to maintain and
develop her individuality? How did these two opposites blend in
such a way that unity was maintained in their home?

We believe the answer lies in the preceding chapter (John
11), when Lazarus died. When word reached Jesus that Lazarus
was sick, he waited two days before going to Bethany. When he
arrived, he was told that Lazarus was dead. The sisters heard
that Jesus was in town. As might be expected, Martha went to
meet him but Mary stayed home! Perhaps the conversation

between Martha and Jesus holds the clue to the change in Martha's attitude.

In this conversation, Jesus revealed himself to Martha, "I am the resurrection and the life" (v. 25). Martha was face-to-face with the person and the power of the Messiah. Even in the middle of her pain (which obviously was more distracting than the earlier failure of Mary not living up to her expectations), Martha responded in faith, "Yes, Lord," she told him, "I believe that you are the Christ, the Son of God, who was to come into the world" (v. 27).

Martha's confession was much more than just intellectual agreement with Jesus' revelation. This was a life-changing encounter that was immediately evident in Martha's attitude toward her sister. In the very next verse we read, "And after she had said this [her confession that Jesus is the Christ], she went back and called her sister, Mary, aside. 'The Teacher is here,' she said, 'and is asking for you'" (v. 28).

We sense a gentleness in Martha as she called Mary aside. Could it be that Martha did not want to embarrass Mary by calling attention to the fact that she had not gone out to meet Jesus? She did not criticize her sister—she simply told Mary that Jesus was asking for her. We wonder if her impatience and resistance toward Mary were washed away in the light of the majesty and unconditional love of the Messiah.

Then Martha witnessed the raising of her brother Lazarus. Again she came face-to-face with the power and sovereignty of the Lord of Glory.

Surely it was the person and the power of Christ that enabled these two women to blend their differences, yet retain their individuality. We see the richness of their relationship in the fact that though their individual uniqueness continued to develop, they did not become individualistic. They blended into a functional family unit. This is an important distinction in our society where individualism is exalted. We are to develop our individual gifts for the common good.

Perhaps Mary was free to quietly meditate on an appropriate act of worship because she had confidence that Martha was caring for the food ministry. Perhaps Martha could concentrate on the meal because she trusted her sister to add the creative touch to the occasion.

When these two women blended their differences to produce the completeness of a delightful meal and a special expression of love, they had the privilege of ministering to Jesus. How restful and encouraging this visit to Bethany must have been for him as he made his way to Calvary. Aren't you glad that he did not have to deal with two bickering women but instead was blessed by their joint ministry?

Our firm belief in the person and power of Christ will enable us to make biblical choices. The Lord of Glory has accepted us, and we can accept others. When women extend acceptance and approval, they create an atmosphere of encouragement where everyone can grow and serve in love.

> I urge you to live a life worthy of the calling you have received. Be completely humble and gentle; be patient, bearing with one another in love. Make every effort to keep the unity of the Spirit through the bond of peace." (Eph. 4:1–3)

NEXT STEPS FOR WOMEN

We need to admit our need for one another. We have heard so much about being self-sufficient and independent that we are often afraid to admit a need for friendships with others. Younger women need to express their desire for the support and approval of older women. Older women need to enter into the lives of younger women and nurture them in Christ. Women in various seasons and circumstances of life need to realize the value of their life experiences and share that perspective with one another.

As women we also must recognize our marvelous capacity for creating an atmosphere of love and acceptance where a spirit of unity can be maintained. We are masters at creating ambience. The church of the Lord Jesus should not be robbed of this gift that women are so uniquely equipped to give.

130

NEXT STEPS FOR MEN IN
OFFICES OF AUTHORITY

The elders in our opening scene experienced both the positive and the negative sides of a woman's ability to create an atmosphere. Realizing how important it is to the entire church for the women to cultivate supportive relationships with one another, they should first spend time praying earnestly for the women.

As the spiritual leaders of the church, they could also offer instruction that would help the women understand their value and their capacity to have a deep impact on building a sense of community. Perhaps a sermon on Titus 2:3–5 would help the older and younger women realize their need for each other. The pastor and one or two elders could also discuss and pray about the situation with a few spiritually mature women.

In any case, the male leadership must not take a hands-off approach. Remember, Paul exhorted Euodia and Syntyche to agree with each other in the Lord, and he asked his loyal yokefellow to help these women agree with each other (Phil. 4:2–3).

STRATEGY FOR THE WOMEN'S MINISTRY

Part of the emphasis of a vital women's ministry should be to facilitate the development of supportive relationships. Classes on relational skills, prayer partners, panel discussions on the needs of women in various seasons and circumstances of life, support groups to meet specific needs, and fellowship and ministry opportunities should all be included in a women's ministry. A healthy women's ministry will be a vehicle to help women connect with and support one another. A healthy women's ministry will go a long way in "keeping mama happy"—as well as everyone else in the church!

LEADERSHIP SKILLS FOR WOMEN

Leaders keep their eyes on long-term goals, on the goals that are bigger than any one program or relationship. They focus on possibilities rather than on obstacles. Leaders are able to say, "what if. . ." whenever others say, "yes, but. . ." If the women in the scenario had focused on what they could contribute, like Mrs. Jackson, rather than on their own needs that were not being met, how different their lives might be.

One thing that leaders can do is to use positive relationship skills to enable others to focus on goals, not obstacles, and to assure that the creativity and leadership of everyone in the group has a chance to surface.

Active Listening

Use rephrasing, probing, questioning, and even silence to encourage others to express themselves fully so that you understand completely both what they are trying to say (content) and the feelings behind what they are saying (emotion). Active listening lets you know precisely what others are thinking and feeling. They will feel valued because you took the time and energy to listen to them.

Empathy

Put yourself in the other person's place. Focus on understanding, not on judging. Too often, we jump to conclusions about the other person's intentions and discount what they are saying because we think we "know where they are coming from." Instead of making negative judgments, good leaders do what R. C. Sproul calls "best-case analysis"—assume that the other person has the very highest motives in taking the position they are taking, and seek to understand them from this point of view.

Responding Supportively

Support begins with careful listening and empathy. Once you have really listened and established empathy, you can honestly say, "I understand your position," even if you don't agree with that position.

Reframing

Just as changing the frame and matting for a painting or poster can dramatically change its appearance, looking at an issue from another point of view can dramatically change the response to it. Reframed statements often begin with phrases like: "Another way to look at this is. . ." or "Let me give you my perspective on that."

These are certainly not the only skills needed to develop positive relationships, but they are the building blocks that can recharge a group with energy and commitment.

SIX MONTHS LATER

At the meeting six months ago, the men wisely addressed the issue of the women's feelings. Later the pastor and two elders met with Mrs. Jackson, the president of the women's ministry, and two other women. Both Mrs. Jackson and the men used active listening skills in order to completely understand each other. Everyone shared their concerns. After much discussion, they found that part of the problem was that many women were lonely and hurting. There were Bible studies for the women, but there was no opportunity for sharing and prayer.

The president of the women's ministry met with the Bible study leaders who listened attentively and responded supportively. They all agreed that time needed to be allocated to develop nurturing relationships. They also discussed ways to help the women bond together. As these ideas were implemented there was a noticeable change in the atmosphere in the church. The elders continued to pray regularly for the women. The women and the elders developed genuine empathy for one another.

Now, six months later, the elders began their meeting with a time of praise and sharing. The pastor rejoiced as he listened.

"My wife is thrilled with the Titus 2:3 ministry. She has been paired with Mrs. Green, and this godly older woman has been such a blessing to her. Mrs. Green prays daily for our children and is always available to listen when my wife needs to talk. Last week, when two of the children were sick, Mrs. Green brought us a meal. You cannot imagine the difference this has made in my wife's attitude."

"I praise the Lord for the prayer ministry of our women. Our family received a card this week from one of the women's Bible study groups saying they prayed for us. It made us feel so loved and accepted."

"My wife had felt so lonely and isolated, but when the women on the encouragement team visited her while she was in the hospital after our baby was born, and then another group brought food when she came home, she was thrilled. Her whole attitude has changed. She is anxious to become involved in the women's ministry."

One of the older men spoke next. "My wife had felt so useless before she was asked to be a part of the encouragement ministry. Now she spends several hours a week calling women who have visited the church. She also gets together with others to pray for these visitors. This has filled a void in her life and has made her feel needed again. She had been thinking that because she no longer has the energy to teach the children that there was no place for her in the ministry of the church. Now she realizes that she was wrong."

The pastor suggested that they go to prayer and, "with one heart and mouth," praise God for the godly women who were willing to invest time and energy into creating an atmosphere and developing ministries where women were bonded to one another. The entire church fellowship was enjoying the blessings!

THE BOTTOM LINE

Does the church need more than Marthas? What do you think? We believe that the church needs more than the first

Martha we met, the Martha who focused on tasks rather than Jesus. But Jesus did not leave Martha there. Through him, she developed her full potential. Martha became a woman whose *focus* gave her the *wisdom* to *confidently* serve others. The *unity* that came from this allowed Martha and those around her to fulfill their potential—to glorify God. The church should not do less. Today's church can provide the environment and the opportunities for all its women to become the new Marthas.

Conclusion

The bottom-line qualification for leadership is for one to have a following. No matter what other credentials a person has, if no one follows, it is quite a stretch to call that person a leader. A helper-leader is one who is ready to lead or follow, to serve or accept service from others. To quiet the voices that lead to pride or arrogance (the ones that say, "You deserve better than this"), and the voices that lead to dependence and failure to use our gifts (the ones that ask "Who do you think you are?" and say, "You can't possibly do this"), requires prayer and support.

A growing helper-leader listens only to the voice of God speaking to her through his Word. She embraces the greatest commandment as defined by her Lord:

> Love the Lord your God with all your heart and with all your soul and with all your mind. This is the first and greatest commandment. And the second is like it: "Love your neighbor as yourself." (Matt. 22:37–39)

The helper-leader lives out this principle of love in such a way that she influences others to follow her ideas and her example. They see that she is focused not on herself, but on Christ.

The helper-follower may not see herself as a leader. Her leadership, however, is evident through her influence on others. For example, a humble, godly grandmother, known to her family and her church as one who loves and lives for her Savior, would never think of herself as being a leader. Yet recently, her granddaughter, Kelli, was featured on a local television station during Drug Awareness Week as being an example of a drug-free teen. After filming Kelli at home with her family, in class, and at cheerleader practice, the camera zoomed in on her vibrant, beautiful face as the reporter asked, "Kelli, why don't you drink or take drugs?" Without a moment's hesitation Kelli's face lit up as she said, "If I were ever tempted to drink or take drugs, I know I would see the face of my Grandmother and I just wouldn't be able to do it." This grandmother, who prays daily for her children and grandchildren, epitomizes the helper-leader who influences others to follow Christ. This grandmother has a following!

This kind of influence comes from submission to the authority of Jesus and from the directions we have been given in the Bible as to how we should live our lives. Most evangelical women have rejected those parts of the feminist movement that are contrary to Holy Scripture. We recognize that God established an order in the world through the roles assigned to each of us. But we feel compelled to sound a warning about listening to the voices of the biblical feminists who say that we must have access to ordination in order to be equal. If we understand them correctly, they tell us that equality and full participation mean that we must be allowed to do the same things that men do. This saddens us, for it devalues what women were designed to contribute to the church. It frightens us, for if we insist on this sameness, the church will be robbed of the completeness that can only come as men and women are fulfilling their assigned roles. We do not have to do the same things as men in order to fully participate.

As we write this, my (Susan's) family is preparing to celebrate the first birthday of our grandchild, Hunter.

I vividly remember that day a year ago when he was born. Gene and I were in the hall outside the delivery room. The nurse came out and gave us hospital gowns and masks. She would tell us nothing. . .but her smile told us that everything was all right.

When we stepped into that delivery room and saw our daughter Kathryn, our son-in-law Dean, and that precious baby, the word that immediately came to my mind was "complete."

Later, as I reflected on this, I realized that these young parents had shared in the excitement of this birth. They had attended childbirth classes, and Dean had been with Kathryn throughout the delivery. They had both fully participated in this birth—though Kathryn would quickly tell you that they had different assignments! They had different roles to play, but they were both focused on the same objective: the birth of their baby. When the task was completed there was a peaceful picture of completeness. They each had words of praise and appreciation for what the other had done.

Can you imagine the reaction of the doctor if they had argued about wanting to do the same thing? Or consider the confusion that would have existed in that delivery room if they had been suspicious of, or competitive with, one another. Think how destructive it would have been if either of them had spent energy trying to rewrite the role assignments so that there was equality. It sounds preposterous, but I'm sure you get the point.

Role differentiation does not mean inequality. I realize that the metaphor of giving birth is incomplete, but consider again the pattern seen in the Trinity where there is equality of person but differentiation of function. In explaining the ministry of the Holy Spirit, Jesus said:

> But the Helper, the Holy Spirit, whom the Father will send in My name, He will teach you all things, and bring to your remembrance all that I said to you. (John 14:26 NASB)

> But when He, the Spirit of truth, comes, He will guide you into all truth; for He will not speak on His own initiative, but whatever He hears, He will speak; and He will disclose to you what is to come. He shall glorify Me; for He shall take of Mine, and shall disclose *it* to you. (John 16:13–14 NASB)

In the Trinity, the person in the role of helper extends this ministry of help by teaching, reminding, and guiding. He does not act on his own initiative nor for his own glory, yet he irresistibly influences God's elect by taking the words of Jesus and speaking them to our hearts so that we can believe and obey. This gentle, unseen Helper is equal with the Father and the Son, though he performs a different function in regard to the salvation of God's people.

Our value is not determined by our role nor our assignment in the kingdom. Our worth is based on the glorious truth that we are image-bearers of the sovereign, triune God of glory. And we bear that image regardless of our circumstances or our roles.

It is time for evangelical men and women to move beyond suspicion and avoidance of one another in ministry to a position of mutual support and appreciation of our different functions in the kingdom. The "present dark ages" (as Charles Colson so aptly describes our current conditions) demand that we move beyond confusion to involved concern if we are going to penetrate this darkness with the light of the Gospel. Kingdom obedience and sanctified social consciousness simply will not allow us to avoid involvement by squandering our energy on suspicion of, or competition with, the opposite sex. By entering into a partnership within the ministry of the church where men and women appreciate, affirm, encourage, and support one another, there will be completeness of ministry that will glorify our Father.

Often we hear the statement, "Men are the head but women are the heartbeat of the church." This may be an old cliche, but it is not worn out—there is still truth in it. Head and heart leadership are needed for balance and completeness in ministry. A head that tries to make decisions and determine direction for a body apart from the lifeblood pumped to it by the heart is ineffective to say the least. When the brain goes without oxygen, which the heart supplies, it soon begins to deteriorate. Likewise if a heart stopped functioning in order to take on the responsibilities of the brain, the body would suffer a heart attack. Both heart and head are absolutely essential not only for a living body, but for a healthy body! A church without head-and-heart leadership is in a precarious situation.

OUR CHALLENGE TO WOMEN

We challenge evangelical women to be pacesetters by leaving behind confusing rhetoric about our roles, and moving ahead to begin meeting needs. Make yourself available to serve the Lord and pray for wisdom to discern his direction. Ask God to develop within you a greater sensitivity to the needs of those he wants you to serve.

We beg you not to use anything in this book as a weapon to fight the men in your church. If you do this, you have completely misunderstood or misinterpreted us. Even if you are in a church that is not addressing the issue of employing women's gifts, we urge you to resolutely refuse to become adversarial. Resolve to offer the winsome help that is needed. Determine by God's grace that you will be the kind of woman described in Proverbs 31—a woman of noble character whose worth is far more than rubies; a woman conducting herself in such a way that the men have full confidence in her; a woman speaking with wisdom and faithful instruction on her tongue.

This woman's husband was respected at the city gate. He was able to function as an effective leader because he had a suitable helper. This book is not about the role of women in the home. However, we must not miss the point that a man's ministry in the church is unquestionably enhanced by the quality of his home life. Men who are loved and encouraged by their wives at home will much more likely have positive feelings toward women at church.

Neither is this book about the role of women as mothers. No challenge to Christian women, however, would be complete without an affirmation of motherhood. If you are privileged to be a mother, the only lifetime assignment given by the Father that has a greater priority (other than your relationship with him) is that of your relationship with your husband. Introducing your children to the Savior and influencing them to live Christianly in a non-Christian culture is an eternal investment worthy of your time and energy.

We urge women who are employed outside the home to

140

develop proficiency in their professions and to bring those skills and experiences back into the church.

We are thrilled with many of our empty-nester sisters who are using their new free time in imaginative ways to channel areas of interest into ministry. Disaster relief, environmental concerns, prison ministries, and cross-cultural outreach are just a few of the issues being addressed by these women. They need Christian sisters to join them.

We are also blessed by the testimony of our empty-nester sisters who have had their expected free time channeled in ways they neither planned nor desired—grandmothers raising grandchildren because of the divorce of their children, women caring for aging parents or invalid husbands, and others who are lovingly ministering to needy family members. They should not be forced to serve in loneliness. We must surround these heroine-helpers with the supportive help and encouragement they need.

Develop your social conscience by learning about ethical issues, particularly those affecting women and children—abortion, pornography, abuse, etc. Then pray about your responsibility in these areas. The victims, the fatherless, the needy, and the afflicted are everywhere. These victims (abandoned and abused women, crack babies, rape victims), the fatherless (orphans, throw-away teens), the needy (the unemployed, the homeless), and the afflicted (those dying, those hurting, the elderly, the lonely), are in desperate need of help. Challenge the women's ministry in your church to pray about ways to address these needs. If there is no organized women's ministry, ask two or three women to join you in praying about this. We can't do everything, but if we all do something, we can make a difference.

Become aware of needs in your community. Is there a significant international population? In many places the mission field has come to our doorsteps through foreign students studying on our campuses and through foreign businesses locating in our communities. International women long for opportunities to be in our homes and to learn of our culture.

Many of these women are from cultures that prohibit interaction with anyone except other women. A women's ministry has unlimited opportunities for friendship evangelism among these women.

When we think about our Christian sisters in America who hold to God's Word as inerrant truth, we visualize the refreshing effects of a gentle breeze blowing across our morally parched land. Jesus uses this wind imagery in John 3 when he talks about the influence of the Holy Spirit. The prayer of our hearts is that Spirit-empowered women will unite to infuse our churches, our communities, and our culture with the fresh, invigorating love of Jesus.

If we could give one assignment it would be to pray. The power of prayer cannot, and must not, be underestimated. It is the single most powerful activity we can undertake. However, this challenge carries a caution: sound theology must be *the* basis for ministry. Unless ministry is an expression of our study of God's Word, we can easily be "swept away by every wind of doctrine" and swept into ministries that express unbiblical philosophies. Develop theological astuteness through systematic study of God's Word, then practice that theology through active involvement in helping others.

OUR CHALLENGE TO MEN

Our challenge to men is not a call to change the structure of your church government, but a request to examine that structure to see if women's gifts are being used to the maximum. Because you have been entrusted with the office of authority in the church, pray for women and provide ways for our gifts to be unleashed for kingdom service.

Do not take the so-called safe position of indifference. Whereas opposition often makes us angry, indifference makes us sad. Pray for sensitivity to our feelings. We do not ask you to totally understand us. . .you are men and we don't expect you to think like women. But we do ask you to listen to us and to care.

142

Your silence is deafening. Please do not leave us to interpret that silence, for quite likely we will misinterpret it. Can we talk?

If your church structure does not permit women to serve on boards, consider having them in advisory capacities so that the female perspective will be represented.

Are women receiving equal recognition and pay for work done within the church? Often a church secretary fulfills responsibilities that in the business world would be assigned to an administrative assistant. If this is the case, give your secretary the title and pay commensurate with her responsibilities.

Are women in denominational or parachurch ministries fulfilling responsibilities that, if done by a man, would receive more pay? This kind of inequity should not be tolerated by Christian men of integrity.

Evangelical seminaries could fill a huge vacuum by designing programs for women that incorporate study in the development and implementation of women's ministries in the local church. There are specialties in youth ministry, why not in women's ministry? A job market needs to be developed for gifted, qualified women to serve in the local church as director of women's ministries. Seminary women should also be trained to counsel women. Many of the unique problems women are facing could be handled more effectively by women.

We need men to be our friends and our advocates. Give more than lip service to our concerns. Take risks to make room for us to do all that we have been created and gifted by our Father to do. We need men to do this for us because we respect your position of headship and we submit to your authority in the church.

OUR CHALLENGE TO ALL OF GOD'S CHILDREN

It was a deliberate decision to put Psalm 34:3 at the beginning of each chapter because God's glory is the overarching theme of this book. Indeed, it must be the driving force of our lives if we are going to be men and women who influence others to follow Jesus. How do we glorify God? *The Catechism for Young Children* answers this question with childlike simplicity: "By loving Him and doing what He commands." Another question addresses the issue of authority for determining how we love and obey God: "Where do you learn how to love and obey God?"—"In the Bible alone."

We urge you to focus the light of Holy Scripture on everything we have said. We are not infallible, but God's Word is. We are sure that before the printing of this book is complete we will wish we had said some things we omitted and had not said some things we did say. We do not expect everyone to agree with everything we have said, but we do ask you to believe that we have made an honest attempt to be faithful to God's Word. It is your responsibility to put everything we said through the grid of God's Word. The Bible is the authoritative Word of God and the only rule for our faith and practice.

No amount of self-effort will produce the profound self-denial that is necessary to place ourselves under the authority of God's Word so that we love him and do what he commands. But what is impossible with us is possible with God. He has given us a Helper who not only influences us but who also enables us to glorify God.

Glorify the LORD with me: Let us exalt His name together. (Psalm 34:3)